TAJ MAHAL

John Lall, a retired member of the Indian Civil Service, was the first Dewan of Sikkim. In the fifties he was Commissioner in Agra, where he resumed his earlier interest in history. He has written a large number of articles on international affairs, and cultural and administrative subjects, and has found both value and enjoyment in Himalayan studies. He contributed to and edited The Himalaya: Aspects of Change.

OTHER LOTUS TITLES :

Boman Desai	*A Woman Madly in Love*
Chaman Nahal	*Silent Life: Memoirs of a Writer*
Duff Hart - Davis	*Honorary Tiger: The Life of Billy Arjan Singh*
Frank Simoes	*Frank Unedited*
Frank Simoes	*Frank Simoes' Goa*
Harinder Baweja (ed.)	*Most Wanted: Profiles of Terror*
J.N. Dixit (ed.)	*External Affairs: Cross-Border Relations*
Mallikarjun Mansur	*Rasa Yatra: My Journey in Music*
Trans. Pt. Rajshekhar Mansur	
M.J. Akbar	*India: The Siege Within*
M.J. Akbar	*Kashmir: Behind the Vale*
M.J. Akbar	*Nehru: The Making of India*
M.J. Akbar	*Riot after Riot*
M.J. Akbar	*The Shade of Swords*
M.J. Akbar	*Byline*
Meghnad Desai	*Nehru's Hero Dilip Kumar: In the Life of India*
Namita Bhandari (ed.)	*India and the World: A Blueprint for Partnership and Growth*
Nayantara Sahgal (ed.)	*Before Freedom: Nehru's Letters to His Sister*
Rohan Gunaratna	*Inside Al Qaeda*
Eric S. Margolis	*War at the Top of the World*
Maj. Gen. Ian Cardozo	*Param Vir: Our Heroes in Battle*
Mushirul Hasan	*India Partitioned. 2 Vols*
Mushirul Hasan	*John Company to the Republic*
Mushirul Hasan	*Knowledge Power and Politics*
Ruskin Bond	*The Green Book*
Saad Bin Jung	*Wild Tales from the Wild*
Satish Jacob	*From Hotel Palestine Baghdad*

FORTHCOMING TITLES :

Dr Verghese Kurien with Gouri Salvi	*I Too Had a Dream*
Aitzaz Ahsan	*The Indus Saga: From Pataliputra to Pakistan*

TAJ MAHAL
THE GLORY OF MUGHAL AGRA

JOHN LALL

PHOTOGRAPHS BY
D.N. DUBE

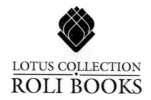

LOTUS COLLECTION
ROLI BOOKS

Lotus Collection

© John Lall 1982
© D N Dube 1982

First published in India 1982
Revised edition 1985 by
Lustre Press Private Limited
New Delhi

This edition published in 2005
The Lotus Collection
An imprint of
Roli Books Pvt. Ltd.
M-75, G.K. II Market, New Delhi 110 048
Phones: ++91 (011) 2921 2271, 2921 2782
2921 0886, Fax: ++91 (011) 2921 7185
E-mail: roli@vsnl.com
Website: rolibooks.com
Also at
Varanasi, Bangalore, Jaipur

ISBN: 81-7436-422-6
Rs. 395

Typeset in Baskerville by Roli Books Pvt. Ltd. and
printed at Presstech Litho Pvt. Ltd., New Delhi

contents

preface

The title of this book declares its own purpose. Stories of the unsurpassed grandeur of the court of the Great Mughals had captivated Western imagination ever since the first European travellers arrived in Agra. From the time it was completed in the middle of the seventeenth century, the Taj Mahal epitomised the glory of Hindustan. It is this Agra that the few pages that follow attempt to portray.

Necessarily, the scene is set in a historical framework. This has involved rigorous selectivity. As Akbar's biographer, Abul Fazl, said: 'Agra was the centre of Hindustan. I have had to stay very close to it.'

The Mughal empire rested on the exertions of two extraordinary men, Babur and Akbar, and the imperial system almost wholly on the latter's energy, breadth of vision and talent for government. Unquestionably, Akbar was one of the

greatest monarchs of all time. Although the name Akbarabad
has fallen into disuse, Agra in its hey day was essentially his
creation, as well as its twin, Fatehpur Sikri.

Enduring as are Akbar's monuments of stone and mortar,
his institutions of government, and particularly his heroic
attempt to banish bigotry from his realm, have a powerful
message for all time. Half Turk half Persian, he gave the
empire a quality of Indianness that ensured its survival for
150 years after his successors had lost the capacity for
governance. Though it was his grandson who built the Taj, this
Indo-Persian gem is the ultimate expression of the syncretic
Indian genius which was sedulously cultivated by the greatest
of the Mughals.

I am deeply indebted to many distinguished people who
have helped in one way or other, though I must alone bear any
responsibility for the book's shortcomings. Dr Satish Chandra,
Professor of History at the Jawaharlal Nehru University,
undertook the thankless task of reading the first two sections of
the manuscript and steering me clear of manifest pitfalls. Dr
W.H. Siddiqui, Superintending Archaeologist, was under siege
for a good part of the time taken in writing. I drew heavily on
his unrivalled knowledge of Agra and Fatehpur Sikri. Dr G.A.
Qamar, caretaker of the Taj for many years, spared long hours
for me in his *haveli* in the old *qasba* of Mumtazabad. Three and
a half centuries ago, Tajganj, as it is now called, was teeming
with architects, builders, designers and workmen for the
twenty-two years taken to build the Taj Mahal. There could be
no better place, and no more knowledgeable person, to initiate
me into the spirit of the times. Mr Nasir-ud-din Malik, Senior

Horticulturist, Mughal Gardens, gave me invaluable information about the old garden. Mr S.P. Srivastava, Superintending Archaeologist at Agra, and his staff, were uniformly helpful.

Special thanks are due to the Director General, the Director of Publications and the Library staff of the Archaeological Survey of India.

Sources were quarried in all kinds of places. My esteemed friends Professor Rafiq Ahmad, Director, Centre for South Asian Studies, Punjab University, Lahore, was able to obtain for me an important article from the 1932 annual issue of *Karwan*. I can only inadequately express my gratitude to the staff of the National Archives and Mr H.K. Kaul, Librarian of the India International Centre. The centre provided an environment unrivalled for quiet study.

NEW DELHI   JOHN LAL
1982

conquest-reconquest

Unknown to the people of Agra, the destiny of their city hung on the issue of a dynastic struggle in Central Asia. The year was 1483. A son had just been born to the wife of Omar Sheikh, the Timurid ruler of Farghana. He was given the name Zahir-ud-din Muhammad, but finding it difficult to pronounce, his father's nobles called him simply Babur, or Tiger.

A name could hardly have suited anyone so well. He needed all the tiger's qualities of noble courage and lightning attack to survive in his precarious inheritance. Set in the jewelled valley of the Sir Darya, Farghana was the envy of neighbouring Tashkent and Samarqand, two other states in the entrancingly beautiful valleys of Transoxiana. It was this Babur who, forty-three years later, recorded a laconic sentence in his memoirs: 'I entered Agra at the Afternoon Prayer of Thursday

(28 Rajab) and dismounted at the *manzil* of Sultan Ibrahim.' It was 10 May 1526. Agra's golden age had begun.

Who were these Central Asians, who, with such suddenness, had taken control of the destinies of Hindustan? Since their conquest turned the course of history, and left its indelible stamp not just on Agra but the country as a whole down to this day, it is necessary to briefly trace this remarkable development.

The Mongols were hardy nomads and pastoralists in the steppes of north-eastern Asia, apparently quite content with their rough existence and shamanistic beliefs. Then, in the thirteenth century, the hordes suddenly errupted from their vast grazing grounds. Chingiz Khan, the spearhead of the first horde, was unquestionably one of the greatest military geniuses of his age. At first the Mongols struck out westwards to the glittering cities of the Tarim basin. One branch swept on to the very gates of Moscow, while another turned southward to bring famed Cathay under heel. Nothing could withstand the furious onslaught of the horsemen with their short swords, arrows and pitiless mien. Even fortified towns fell to their siege engines.

Having subdued most of Asia and much of Europe, the Mongols were in turn subdued, but in a totally different way. These ruthless conquerors had celebrated victories by slaughtering their foes and erecting towers of heads on the battlefields. In time, however, they yielded to the very civilisation which, politically and militarily, they had so completely destroyed. One of the strangest twists in history is that these barbarians became the carriers of the civilisations they absorbed.

2

Transoxiana, the cool green valleys between the Amu and the Sir Daryas, the Oxus and Jaxartes of old, had been fertilised through the ages by cultural streams flowing with Buddhism from India, and back into the same cultural matrix from China, and later and most powerfully by the Islamic culture of Persia. It was here that local Turkish rulers set themselves up in the name of the Mongol Il – Khans. Thus it was that Timur, a Chaghatai chieftain of the Barlas tribe, proclaimed himself Grand Amir in the year 1369. His formidable military exploits won him an empire that stretched across West Asia, from the Sir Darya to the Mediterranean Sea. In 1398, Timur, the scourge of Central Asia, descended with his horsemen to the plains of Hindustan, conquered the Punjab, and put Delhi to the sword. The fabulous loot with which he staggered away has not been forgotten in Hindustan; but a far uglier memory was the massacre of tens of thousands of citizens in the capital city.

Babur was a direct descendant of Timur and distantly connected with Chingiz Khan through the female line. When he launched his invasion in November 1525, he made use of his former relationship in laying claim to Timur's conquests in the Punjab. Babur himself, like Timur, was a Turk. The dynasty he founded was the House of Timur, but the misleading name Mughal, derived from the Mongol conquerors of Asia, came to include the Turks, the Mongols and other Central Asian tribes who accompanied the rulers from the hills and valleys of Turkestan. It has clung to them to this day. The Afghans alone remained a distinct group, retaining their separate identity.

However successful they were in war, the rulers of Turkestan failed to establish a unified state. They were constantly at war with each other. When Omar Sheikh died in 1494, his eleven-year-old son Babur was proclaimed king of Farghana. Young as he was, the Uzbeg chief Shaibani Khan gave him no peace. Samarqand, his ancestor Timur's capital and the greatest prize of all, was won and lost again. The long drawn out dynastic struggles in Turkestan at the end of the fifteenth and the early part of the sixteenth century eventually forced Babur to seek his fortune in Afghanistan. A relative, who sat insecurely on the throne of Kabul, had appealed for help. The excuse was just what Babur needed to make him turn away from his beloved Farghana. In 1504, with a small force of 4000 men desperate for action and plunder, he crossed the Hindu Kush and captured the fort of Kabul. Timur's young descendant needed a stepping-stone to further ventures and a safe all-back position where he could recuperate before striking out again. Kabul admirably suited both purposes.

Babur had never really abandoned hopes of regaining his lost dominions in Turkestan. In 1511, he managed to recover Samarqand where he was joyously received by the inhabitants of Timur's capital. But fortune smiled only briefly. Babur could not compete with the rising power of Shah Ismail of Persia; even the modest hope of conquering Badakshan had to be given up. Raids into Hindustan seemed a far easier proposition. The passes through which, over the centuries, Aryans, Greeks, Huns and Afghans had descended from the mountains, echoed with the hooves of his horses as he rode four times through its inviting plains. The loot with which he

4

returned sharpened the appetite of his followers, who too were eager for more. To Babur's discerning eye the country's disunity invited intervention. He was convinced that with a concerted effort the prize of Hindustan could be his.

The twenty-two long year before Babur launched his full-scale invasion of Hindustan was a time of preparation. In 1514, the Ottoman Turks had defeated the Shah of Persia using the new-fangled weapon of artillery. The implications were not lost on Babur. He engaged a Rumi (Ottoman) gunner and matchlockmen and mastered the Turkish order of battle, later to be used with devastating effect in two critical battles in Hindustan. This was the *tulughma*, which essentially consisted of probing charges to the enemy's rear, while lashed guns and matchlockmen held firm in the centre.

In good time, affairs in Delhi and the Punjab gave him a handle. He raised the claim of lawful dominion derived from Timur's conquest and descended through the defiles in November 1525 with a picked force of 12,000 horsemen. It was the largest he had ever led, and he was joined by dissidents in the Punjab. Kamran, his younger son, was with Babur, while Humayun, the eldest, joined him from Badakshan, but not before Babur had written 'harsh letters ... lecturing him severely because of the long delay beyond the time fixed for him to join me.' Even at so critical a time, and under so severe a taskmaster, Humayun betrayed the fatal weakness that was to cost him the throne in 1540.

Skirmishes in the Punjab with Daulat Khan Lodi and other Afghan chiefs detained Babur for a while. It was not until April 1526 that his tiny force confronted Sultan Ibrahim's army

5

of 1,00,000 men and 1,000 elephants on the plain of Panipat, about eighty kilometres north of Delhi. A week went by waiting for the Hindustani host to attack. On 24 April, Friday (8 Rajab), 'news came when it was light enough to distinguish one thing from another that the enemy was advancing in fighting array. We at once put on mail, armed and mounted,' recalled Babur in his memoirs.

His orders on the battlefield read like a model exercise and reveal his qualities as one of the greatest field commanders of the age. 'Our orders were for the turning-parties to wheel from right and left to the enemy's rear, to discharge arrows and to engage in the fight; and for the right and left (wings) to advance and join battle with him. The turning-parties wheeled round and began to rain arrows down.' Three commanders were ordered to engage the centre. 'From that same position Ustad Aliquli (the master gunner) made good discharge of *feringhi* shots ... Our right, left, centre and turning-parties having surrounded the enemy, rained arrows down on him and fought ungrudgingly.' Babur concludes his account of the battle with the well-known words: 'By God's mercy and kindness, this difficult affair was made easy for us! In one half-day, that armed mass was laid upon the earth. Five or six thousand men were killed in one place close to Ibrahim. Our estimate of the other dead, lying all over the field, was 15 to 16,000, but it came to be known, later in Agra from the statements of Hindustanis, that 40 or 50,000 may have died in that battle.'

Babur's great victory must have stunned the people of Hindustan with its decisiveness. Over a hundred years earlier, Timur, with the ruthlessness of the early Turks, had sacked, pillaged and killed, and returned to Samarqand. For Babur there was no return. He could not afford to alienate his new subjects; his victory was not stained by ruthless carnage. Babur held together his motley horde of Turks, Uzbegs and Afghans with a mixture of firmness and understanding and inspired them with his own daring leadership and personal bravery. Thorough training and the *feringhi* pieces under Ustad Aliquli, combined with sound tactics, had triumphed on the battlefield. Babur's restraint in victory was to win him the more certain conquest of permanent dominion.

Babur moved briskly to consolidate his gains. There was no time to be lost. The sun had not set on the field of battle before he had sent off two detachments to Delhi and Agra with orders to mount guard over the treasuries. Humayun and a troop of leading *begs* (dignitaries) and horsemen were appointed 'to ride fast and light to Agra.'

For himself, Babur reined in his horse in Delhi to observe the prescribed ceremony of kingship, and to honour the tombs of Nizam-ud-din Auliya and other saints. This was no empty ritual. While he stayed behind in camp on the outskirts of the old capital of Hindustan, his emissaries went into Delhi for the congregational prayer. They read the *khutba* (Friday's midday prayer) in his name, and distributed money to the poor and needy. With the blessings of Allah, the new *padshah* was proclaimed in the assembly of the faithful. It was only after this formal assumption of kingship that he hastened to join Humayun in Agra.

For centuries, Agra had been a place of only secondary importance. Its immediate capture had become vital to the stability of Babur's dominion in Hindustan, because of changes in the power structure in the region since the start of the sixteenth century. In the early medieval period, the Rajputs built a fort there which was called Badalgarh (Cloud Touching Fort). In 1504, Sultan Sikandar Lodi transferred his capital to Agra and stored his treasure in the fort. When Babur joined Humayun there, the main power centre in Hindustan fell into his hands.

The family of Raja Bikramjit of Gwalior, who was killed at Panipat, gave Humayun 'a mass of jewels ... amongst which was the famous diamond,' the Koh-i-noor. It remained with the House of Timur until the sack of Delhi by Nadir Shah of Persia in 1739. Eventually it fell into the hands of Maharaja Ranjit Singh of the Punjab. When they annexed the province, the British sent the diamond to Queen Victoria, and it has remained with the Crown Jewels ever since.

Babur's glorious victory and the capture of the dead sultan's fabulous treasure had not reconciled his followers to the prospect of staying on in Hindustan. They were bent on returning to Kabul. Agra in May was an inferno. To make matters worse its inhabitants had fled in terror; there was neither food for his men nor fodder for their horses. Babur had to lure them into staying with largess that was breathtaking in its lavishness. Humayun was given no less than 70 lakhs[1] and 'a treasure house was bestowed on him ... without ascertaining its contents.' Friends, relatives, and others great and small in Kabul and Central Asia were sent gifts of coins, gold and silver, jewels, slaves, and even dancing girls from the sultan's harem. Babur's daughter Gulbadan Begum complained that he impoverished himself. And the historian Ferishtra tells us that he was nick-named Qalandar (destitute).

But even this splendid generosity was not enough. It was a time of great anxiety. Once again, however, as on the battlefield, Babur was equal to the occasion. He summoned his *begs* to the old fort of Badalgarh and addressed them in the stirring words reproduced in his memoirs: 'By the labours of several years, by encountering hardship, by long travel, by flinging myself and the army into battle and by deadly slaughter, we, through God's grace, beat these masses of enemies in order that we might take their broad lands. And now what force compels us, what necessity has arisen that we should, without cause, abandon countries taken at such risk of life? Was it for us to remain in Kabul, the sport of harsh poverty? Henceforth, let no well-wisher of mine speak of such things! But let not those turn back from going, who, weak in strong persistence, have set their faces to depart!'

Babur's impassioned eloquence won the day. It was a historic victory, the real turning point in the history of medieval India. Thenceforth, the Mughal invaders were committed to the occupation of Hindustan.

Babur has left a remarkably perceptive appreciation of the varied conditions of Hindustan and his own still precarious military position. The *'rais* and rajas' in the vicinity were easily accounted for, but the biggest threat by far was the Rajput confederacy under the renowned Rana Sanga of Mewar. The Rana had lost an arm and an eye and carried eighty scars of battle on his body. The flower of Rajput chivalry flocked to his standard, and he was joined by Hasan Khan Mewati and

9

Afghan remnants. Babur's estimate was that 201,000 men confronted his miniscule army at Kanwaha near Sikri on 17 March 1527. It was the last great Rajput stand against the Mughals before the new conquerors themselves became the champions of Hindustan.

Babur's 'holy warriors of Islam' carried out a copybook repetition of the tactics that had won them the day at Panipat. Their foes 'dispersed like carded wool before the wind, and like moths scattered abroad.' The day ended with a characteristic Mongol-Turki victory celebration. 'Mounds were made of the bodies slain, pillars of their heads.' As for Babur, 'Thanks be to God!' he exclaimed; 'a *ghazi* I became.' The Rana escaped, only to die the following year.

Even after disposing of the Rajputs, Babur knew no rest in the remaining three and a half years of his life. He remained a Central Asian at heart and seems to have planned to return to Kabul without abandoning his conquests in Hindustan. Nothing came of these plans. Humayun had fallen seriously ill. His mother, Maham Begum, brought her sick son to Agra where the drama of the great renunciation was to be enacted. Accounts have been given both by Babur's daughter, Gulbadan Begum, and Akbar's biographer, Abul Fazl.

The prince's fever did not respond to treatment. As a last resort, Mir Abu Baqa, a well-known saint, suggested that the emperor should make an offering of something of great value. It was hinted that the great diamond Koh-i-noor might be appropriate; but in a dramatic gesture Babur declared that the prince could surely not value anything more than his own father's life.

10

He prayed for divine intercession, circling three times round Humayun's bed: 'O God! if a life may be exchanged for a life, I, who am Babur, give my life and my being for Humayun.' According to Gulbadan, fever took hold of Babur the same day, while Humayun poured water on his own head and came out and gave audience. A miracle indeed, though the rite of self-renunciation was not unknown in those times.

Whether it was this fever that finally took Babur away is in doubt. He survived a few months and died on 25 December 1530, with symptoms resembling those that appear after poisoning. A herald dressed in red, seated on an elephant, went through the streets of Agra announcing that the emperor had become a dervish, leaving the throne to Humayun Mirza. Four days later, on 29 December, the *khutba* was read in Humayun's name. It was the first Mughal succession in Agra, and the only one destined to be peaceful and undisputed. But Humayun failed to rise to the responsibilities of a sovereign. In ten years he had lost all that his valiant and tireless father had won in Hindustan.

Babur's body was laid in the Gul-afshan garden in Agra, which had been his retreat from the cares of state. But it was only a temporary resting place, for he had willed that he should be buried in an open grave in his favourite garden in Kabul. It was not until after Humayun's defeat at Chausa in 1539, when the tide had definitely turned against him, that Babur's remains were taken to Kabul and interred in a garden facing the snows of the Paghman range. The simple memorial conveyed its own eloquent message, but Shah Jahan could not resist the inclination to build, and to him is attributed the beautiful mosque near the grave. Jahangir, always the lover of the poetic, is believed to have ordered the inscription of the lines on the upright stone memorial: 'When Paradise became his dwelling and Razwan (Doorkeeper of Paradise) asked me the date, I gave him for an answer, "Paradise is forever Babur *Padshah*'s abode".'

Babur was indeed Firdaus Makani (Dweller in Paradise), the name by which he was known after his death.

***

The conquests in Hindustan which Babur had left to the care of his son, Humayun, were soon exposed to a looming threat. Sher Khan, an Afghan soldier of fortune, had struck out on his own in Bihar. The storm he had raised in the east was swirling westwards, threatening the throne itself.

At one time the emperor lost his horse while escaping across the river Ganga at Chausa and was saved by the providential help of a water-carrier. Humayun's gratitude was expressed in outlandish exuberance. His sister, Gulbadan Begum, tells the story: 'In those days His Majesty had a certain servant, a water-carrier. As he had been parted from his horse in the river at Chausa, this servant betook himself to his help and got him safe and sound out of the current, His Majesty now seated him on the throne. The name of that menial person we did not learn; some said Nizam, some said Sambal. But to cut the story short, His Majesty made the water-carrier servant sit on the throne, and ordered all the amirs to make obeisance to him. The servant gave everyone what he wished, and made appointments. For as much as two days the emperor gave royal

12

power to that menial.' Humayun's brother, Kamran, was aghast. Princess Gulbadan tells us that he sent a message to His Majesty: 'Gifts and favours of some other kind ought to be the servant's reward. What propriety is there in seating him on the throne? At a time when Sher Khan is near, what kind of affair is this to engage in Your Majesty?'

Gulbadan Begum recounts the story with a straight face. The ladies of the household would never have dreamt of questioning the emperor's whims, but quite obviously the entire family was scandalised by the spectacle of a water-carrier dispensing favours from the throne of Agra. The citizens of the town must have looked askance at these strange goings on. Humayun, who never really had a grip on affairs of state, diverted himself by a display of authority as hollow as it was ridiculous. Sher Khan chased him out of Agra and for three years after that he was in desperate straits, emperor of little more than the horse on which he fled from one refuge to another.

The scene shifts from Agra to the borderlands of Sind and the *subah* of Kabul, but the events are germane to the story of Agra because a child, born while Humayun was in exile, was destined to be the greatest of all the Mughals. In the midst of his troubles, the fugitive emperor's eye fell on Hamida Bano Begum, daughter of Mir Baba Dost, a Persian on his brother Kamran's staff. Humayun pursued her with his unwelcome attentions. Gulbadan Begum puts it like this: 'To cut the story short: for forty days the begum resisted and discussed and disagreed. At last Her Highnes my mother, Dildar Begum, advised her, saying, "after all you will marry someone. Better than a king, who is there?" The begum said, "Oh yes, I will marry someone, but he will be a man whose collar my hand can touch, and not one whose skirt it does not reach." Then my mother again gave her much advice. At last, after forty days, ... His Majesty took the astrolabe into his own blessed hand and, having chosen a propitious hour, summoned Mir Abu Baqa and ordered him to make fast the marriage bond ...'

Humayun's persistence was rewarded. His Persian bride bore him a son at Amarkot in Sind on 15 October 1542. The boy was named Jalal-ud-din Muhammad Akbar, in accordance with an inspiration which had come to him in a dream.[2]

Humayun's tribulations were very far from coming to an end. Virtually bereft of all save his honour, the occasion nevertheless called for a little ceremony. His ewer bearer Jauhar, who has left a revealing account of the years of exile, tells us that the emperor made him fetch a bag, which he always carried. From it Humayun drew a pod of musk. He 'then called for a China plate, and having broken the pod of musk, distributed it among all the principal persons, saying, "this is all the present I can afford to make to you on the birth of my son, whose fame will I trust be one day expanded all over the world, as the perfume of musk now fills this apartment." After the ceremony the drums were beaten, and the trumpets proclaimed the auspicious event.'

Even worse was the treachery by which Humayun was surrounded. Kamran, who was governor of Kabul, had ambitions of his own and insisted on the *khutba* being read in his name. In the swings of fortune, the boy Akbar was captured by his uncles. The luckless emperor made his way to Persia

14

where he was generously treated by Shah Tahmasp. His sister commented, 'The friendship and concord of those two high-placed *pashas* was as close as two nut-kernels in one shell.' Shah Tahmasp fitted out his 'brother' Humayun to take Kabul and was doubtless relieved to see him go. Akbar, then about two-years-old, was exposed by his heartless uncles over the ramparts of Kabul fort when it was invested by Humayun's forces. His chief nurse, Maham Anaga, heroically shielded him from matchlock fire, an act of devotion which had an important influence in the early years of Akbar's rule.

Father and son were reunited when the fort was taken, and Kamran captured and brought before Humayun. Earlier, Humayun had shrunk from the promptings of his followers to do away with his faithless brother. According to Jauhar, in Lahore he had protested: 'No, never for the vanities of the perishable world, will I imbrue my hands in the blood of my brother, but will ever remember the dying words of our respected parent, who said to me, "O Humayun beware, beware, do not quarrel with your brothers, nor ever form any evil intentions towards them," these words are engraved on my heart forever.'

Since then Kamran had repeatedly proved his treachery. The nobles insisted on retribution. Gulbadan Begum describes the scene: 'To make an end of words, one and all urgently set forth: "It is well to lower the head of the breachers of a kingdom."' Even then Humayun could not bring himself to yield to their wishes until they gave it in writing. 'When he drew near to Rohtas,' the princess writes, 'the emperor gave an order to Sayyid Muhammad: "Blind Mirza Kamran in both

15

eyes." The Sayyid went at once and did so.'[3] Hindal had already been killed in a fight while the other brother, Askari, was banished and not heard of again. Humayun was thus left as sole claimant to Babur's conquests, which earlier he had lost through his own folly.

Four years later Humayun braced himself for the reconquest of Hindustan. The circumstances were at last propitious. Sher Khan, with the title of Sher Shah Sur, had ruled for barely five years. In his short reign, he had distinguished himself by his exceptional talent for government. His successors were men of inferior calibre. After his death, Hindustan was racked by internecine conflict. Taking advantage of the confused conditions in the northern part of his former dominions, Humayun reentered Delhi on 23 July 1555. On 24 January 1556, he heard the call to prayer while he was in his library in Purana Qila. Rising for *namaz*, he slipped on the narrow stairs and plunged to his death. As the historian Lane-Poole puts it, Humayun tumbled out of life as he had tumbled through it, leaving his thirteen-year-old son, Akbar, with a claim to the throne though very little by way of material resources to assert his right, except his redoubtable Turki general, Bairam Khan. Young as he was, Akbar was firm in the saddle, adept with bow and arrow and already a fierce swordsman. He was in the Punjab when news of his father's death was received, and was hastily crowned in a mango grove at Kalanaur near Gurdaspur. Bairam Khan now turned his attention to the most formidable threat to the Mughals in the person of the Sur's Hindu general, Himu.

Advancing from Gwalior, with the title of Vikramaditya,

Himu took Agra and marched to Delhi where the Mughal governor was put to flight. The outlook for the young emperor was decidedly bleak. Himu had been joined by 50,000 Afghan and Rajput cavalry and boasted a massive force of 1,500 elephants. To all appearances it was the army of Hindustan confronting an invading force. Once again the armies clashed at Panipat. A chance arrow shot Himu in the eye and threw his forces into confusion, and Bairam Khan's generalship put the prize of Delhi in Akbar's hand. He was destined to become the most celebrated Indian ruler since Ashoka and Chandragupta. Though he had no Indian blood in his veins, Akbar was the first truly national ruler since the Muslim dynasties established themselves in Hindustan in the twelfth century.

The reconquest of Hindustan committed the Mughals to permanent dominion in India. Babur's heart had been in Kabul, and even more so in Samarqand. He would not have abandoned his conquests in the manner of his ancestor Timur, but the Paghman range overlooking Kabul called insistently. In the early days he had counted no less than thirty-three varieties of tulips growing wild in the foothills. Gul-afshan Charbagh in Agra was a poor substitute. Though he had devised water channels there, he could not dispel the fascination of the villages of Istalif and Astarghach, with their incomparably clear and cool running waters, nestling in the shade of the plane trees, nor the charm of the oaks and the spectacular arghwan (Judas tree, *Cercis siliquastrum*) blazing the hillsides with their fiery gold.

Babur's ambivalence about his conquests remained unresolved. He died too soon. Humayun was the sport of circumstances he was unable to control. If he had not been

17

accidentally killed, it is quite likely that he would have preferred Delhi to Agra. A beginning was being made to set up a capital in the area of Dinpanah, where his tomb now is. Even Akbar seemed at first to be undecided. The pacification of the Punjab, his marriage to Muhammad Abdulla Khan's daughter and a sudden passion for the unfamiliar sport of riding elephants, engaged much of his time. He had spent six months in Delhi — perhaps the first settled period in his life — and then took his court to Agra.

Nowhere in Abul Fazl's monumental biography is there more than a hint of the motive for Akbar's decision. He speaks of it as 'the sublime reunion.' Though the Mughals had spent only fourteen years in Agra and had been driven out of it by the usurper Sher Shah, it must have seemed to them that historical justice demanded their return to precisely the same place. This is where, once again, 'the sublime standards' would be unfurled above the battlements of Badalgarh fort. On 30 October 1558, says Abul Fazl, 'the crescent moon standards of the *shahinshah* emerged from the ascension point of the horizon of the city of Agra, and made that fortunate and auspicious city the centre of the circle of the throne ... His Majesty the *shahinshah* gave celestial rank to the citadel, which was known by the name of Badalgarh, by alighting there.' The disgrace of defeat and exile had been wiped out.

---

1 Presumably *dams*, forty of which were equivalent to a rupee. The rupee was equivalent to 2 s. 3 d, so that the gift amounted to £19,687.10 s., a considerable sum at that time.

2   Both Abul Fazl and Khwaja Nizam-ud-din Ahmad say that Akbar was
    born on Sunday the fifth of the month (15 October, 1542) (Rajab AH
    949). Humayun's personal servant, Jauhar, on the other hand, says that
    Akbar was born on the night of the full moon of the month of Shah'ban
    'in consequence of which His Majesty was pleased to name the child (the
    full moon of religion) Badr-ud-din Muhammad Akbar.' But his name
    meant Jalal-ud-din (the glory of religion). Vincent Smith accepted the
    date given by Jauhar, holding that since he was both close to the emperor
    and present at the time, his version must be genuine. The difference in
    the meaning of the child's name suggests inconsistencies in Jauhar's
    account, and there is no satisfactory reason why two important official
    historians should have concealed the real date of birth.

3   There is a detailed account of the whole grisly business in *Tezkereh al*
    vakiat by Jauhar who describes himself as a domestic of the Emperor
    Humayun. The unfortunate Kamran's eyes were pierced by a lancet no
    less than fifty times, after which salt and lemon juice were squeezed into
    them. (*Tezkereh al vakiat,* trans. Maj. Charles Stewart John Murray,
    London, 1832, p.106).

the age of splendour

Agra was the second capital of Hindustan from 1504 to 1658. Abul Fazl called it Dar-ul-Khilafat and Delhi, the traditional capital, Dar-ul-Sultanat. During this span of 154 years, three dynasties ruled from Agra and as many as eleven rulers sat upon the *masnad*. The Lodi Sultans, Sikandar and Ibrahim, were followed by the first two Mughals, Babur and Humayun. The usurper Sher Shah was the first of the Sur dynasty which produced four rulers in the fifteen years following 1540.

In 1555, the Mughals returned from Kabul and revived a claim to the empire which was confirmed the next year after a hotly contested battle at Panipat. Humayun's death left the throne to Akbar, who in turn was succeeded by Jahangir and Shah Jahan. In 1658, Aurangzeb confined his father Shah Jahan in his own marble palace in Agra fort and took away the court to the traditional capital of Delhi.

Strangers in Hindustan

There could hardly have been five men more different than the first Mughal emperors, and for that matter the sixth, Aurangzeb. Yet each made a distinct contribution to the evolutions, in the sixteenth and seventeenth centuries, of the most splendid court in Asia.

Babur never lived to see more than the first gleam of the glorious empire of which he was the founder. To the end he retained the personal unaffectedness that had characterised the strenuous circumstances of his early life. Humayun's reign suffered from occasional suggestions of comic opera; but his humanity, capacity for affection and sheer lovableness of character compensated for lack of judgement. It was left to Akbar to build an enduring edifice on the insecure foundations left to him. He was aided, it is true, by the turmoil and divisions in Hindustan, yet nothing could have withstood his masterful sense of empire. He was, par excellence, the Grand Mughal. His fame spread to the most distant corners of the civilised world. Western rulers sent ambassadors, merchants clamoured for trade; jewellers tempted the nobles with bric-a-brac that they hoped to exchange for gems from the fabled wealth of the orient; physicians, soldiers of fortune, charlatans and priests endured the privations of the long sea voyage and the even more hazardous journey by land to the distant court in Agra. As long as the Mughal emperors were there, Agra witnessed an

The Taj Mahal is a glorious culmination of the artistic fusion of Indian architecture and Moghul ornamentation. It was built over a period of twenty-two years (1632-54), with a labour force of approximately 20,000 workers, at a monumental cost that has never been precisely tabulated. The work was supervised by experienced architects like Makramat Khan and Mir Abdul Karim, though there can be no doubt that the ultimate vision and guidance was Shah Jahan's alone.

Mumtaz Mahal (1593-1631), was the favourite wife of Emperor Shah Jahan. Born Arjumand Banu, she first met Shah Jahan when she was just fourteen years old in a monthly bazaar held in the palace premises. It was love at first sight for both and Shah Jahan promptly secured his father's assurance for her hand in marriage. After marriage she became Shah Jahan's constant, loyal and faithful companion, bearing him fourteen children, of which only seven survived. She died prematurely and tragically in the nineteenth year of their marriage, during childbirth.

Shah Jahan (1592-1666), the Grand Moghul, met Arjumand Banu when he was fifteen, married her when he was twenty and remained in love with her till their last days together. He rewarded her exceptional loyalty by giving her the title of Mumtaz Mahal, or Chosen One of the Palace and the sole authority to use the Royal Seal. She encouraged him in his passion for architecture. Though she only survived long enough after his coronation to see the ongoing reconstruction in marble of the Khas Mahal in the Agra Fort, her demise spurred him to construct in her memory the magnificient Taj Mahal.

An aerial view of the Taj Mahal, framed between the Jamuna to its north and the Charbagh garden to its south. Visible in the background is the sandstone gateway to the Taj.

The translucent marble changes colour with the changing quality of light.

Below: A view of the chamferred corners and the minarets.

Reflecting as many moods as the phases of the day.

Below: Utterly captivating on a shimmering full moon night.

بسم الله الرحمن الرحيم

يا حي يا قيوم برحمتك استغيث

قال الله تبارك وتعالى الذي

والله و اثم ا

The cenotaphs of Shah Jahan and Mumtaz Mahal surrounded by a marble screen in the large octagonal memorial chamber.

Facing page: The 99 names of Allah on Mumtaz Mahal's tomb.

Below: On the head of illuminated sepulchre of Mumtaz Mahal is inscribed a passage from the Koran 'God is He beside whom there is no god. He knoweth what is concealed and what is manifest. He is merciful and compassionate.'

The image of the Taj mirrored in the slow waters of the Jamuna to the north.

The Taj is a monument of the most perfect proportions and from all sides looks the same. The mausoleum is completely constructed in marble and set on a square plinth with four slender minarets.

Below: The translucent marble changes colour with the changing quality of light.

To many, the grandeur of the Taj is complemented by the slender minarets on octagonal bases at the four corners of the marble plinth, detached from the central structure. Built of white marble, each minaret is 133 feet in height, of the most perfect proportions, and surmounted by a splendid cupola supported on eight elegant pillars, reached by a spiral staircase now closed to visitors.

An early morning view of the mausoleum, as the sun rises over yet another day. Eternal in the sands of time, it

age of unexampled splendour. Even after the glory had faded,
it never ceased to cast its spell.

These dazzling years witnessed the burgeoning of the
Central Asian heritage of culture and learning and institutions
of government in the soil of Hindustan. It had already been
made receptive by four hundred years of Muslim rule. What
followed was a two-way evolution. The first was the
Islamicization of the elite culture, or the progressive adoption
of the norms of the Islamic world, which at that time was
dominated by the models of Safavid Persia. The second was
the gradual assimilation of the totality of the Islamic inheritance
in the Indian experience. The contribution made by Indian
thought and culture was encouraged by Akbar and Jahangir.
Both processes were at work in Agra in the age of splendour.
The Mughal city became the crucible, the chance laboratory of
this great experiment in cultural chemistry that ultimately
yielded the composite culture of India.

Babur had achieved his immediate aim of conquest, but it
is rather as an outstanding examplar of Central Asian
civilisation that he left his indelible stamp on Hindustan. The
twentieth century concept of 'roots' applies with special force
to the padshah, who was proclaimed at Friday prayers in Delhi
a few days after Panipat. Unlike his maternal ancestors
Chaghatai and Chingiz Khan, Babur was no pitiless killer.
Though the Mongol tradition never quite died out, it was the
Timurid heritage of culture and learning that Babur brought
with him to Hindustan. Moreover, outstanding as he was as its
torch-bearer he was only the foremost of the cultural stream
that came with him – the *begs* who fought by his side, the ladies

of the harem, and the *khwajas*, men of letters and soldier-administrators who poured in behind him once the Mughal standards were raised over the old fort of Badalgarh. Despite subsequent borrowings from Hindustan, from the very start theirs was the dominant culture. The age of splendour they established cannot be appreciated without an understanding of its roots in Mawara-un-nahr, the lands beyond the Oxus.

Babur himself is the surest guide on this journey into the past, and quite the most delightful. The *Babur Nama* (his diary), written in the heat and passion of experience, but never in despair, is the truest mirror of the times. He wrote in his native Turki in which he was an accepted master, and his translator, Annette S. Beveridge, has admirably succeeded in bringing to life the animation of his style. Unhappily the surviving Turki text covers only eighteen of the forty-seven years of his tumultuous life. In 1589, Akbar directed Abdur Rahim to translate the *Babur Nama* into Persian. Artists of the imperial atelier were commissioned to illustrate it with miniatures, of which many priceless folios have survived in the copy preserved at the National Museum in Delhi.

Abdur Rahim's translation is a tribute to the tradition of scholarship that flourished under the active patronage of Babur's grandson, Akbar. The translator was the son of Akbar's great Turki general, Bairam Khan. He had been cared for by the emperor and became a celebrated soldier and scholar, who rose to the highest rank of *Khan-i-Khanan*. As if that was not enough, he was a distinguished poet in the country's vernacular, Hindi. Abdur Rahim was thus an outstanding example of the renaissance of learning and

24

culture stimulated by the presence of the early Mughals in Hindustan.

In his diary, Babur repeatedly extols the delights of Mawara-un-nahr. Of Samarqand, he says, 'Few towns in the whole habitable world are so pleasant.' It had been adorned by Babur's two great ancestors, Timur and Ulugh Beg, with many fine mosques, *khanqas, madrasas* and tombs, all superb examples of the fifteenth century Central Asian renaissance. In the walled town, Babur says, Timur had built 'a Friday mosque of stone: On this worked many stone-cutters brought from Hindustan.'

Along with the massive plunder in his baggage trains, Timur also took away those of the renowned stone-cutters of Delhi who had not hidden themselves in terror of the Central Asian conqueror. Babur must have recalled this when he established himself in Hindustan. Even in the four short years of his reign he started work on a number of gardens and buildings, and gave clear proof of his passion for architecture.

Babur's immediate reaction to Agra was one of disgust. He remained unreconciled, almost hostile, to it to the very end. 'Hindustan,' he laments in his disarmingly candid memoirs, 'is a country of few charms. Its people have no good looks; of social intercourse, paying and receiving visits there is none; of manners none.' And, characteristically, for the sportsman and lover of nature that he was, 'there are no good horses, no good dogs, no grapes, musk melons or first rate fruits, no ice or cold water, no good bread or cooked food in the bazaars, no hot-baths, no colleges, no candles, torches or candlesticks.'

Even for a diary, Babur's condemnation was as thorough as it could be. But it could hardly have been otherwise. For a Turk from the verdant valleys of Transoxiana, who had been hardened by the harsh winters of Kabul, Agra in the scorching month of May was far from being an inviting haven. 'Three things oppressed us in Hindustan,' he declared, 'its heat, its violent winds, its dust.' Yet he was quick to find a solution. 'Against all three the bath is a protection, for in it, what is known of dust and wind? And during the heats it is so chilly that one is almost cold.' But if the bath provided physical relief from Agra's well-known scourges, it was even more important that the mind should be refreshed and the spirit revitalised.

For Babur, flowers and gardens had been a never failing source of delight. A few days after distributing Sultan Ibrahim's treasure, he crossed over from the crowded city side of the river to the other bank to look for a suitable site. The prospects were exceedingly discouraging. 'Those grounds,' he says in his memoirs, 'were so bad and unattractive that we traversed them with a hundred disgusts and repulsions.' It was Babur's passion for beauty disciplined by order that established the formal garden, enlivened by sparkling water, as the dominant style. The *begs* followed the emperor's lead. 'The people of Hind,' says Babur, 'who had never seen grounds planned as symmetrically and thus laid out, called the side of the Jun (river Yamuna) where (our) residences were, Kabul.' To have created a Kabul in Agra was for Babur the cultural complement of his conquests. It was not just an aesthetic pose, an effort in nostalgia, by a Central Asian longing for the delights of his homeland, but a necessary condition of life.

Order went with beauty, comfort with zest for life. In Agra itself, Babur laid out two such gardens — Zar-afshan (Gold-scattering) and Gul-afshan (Flower-scattering). Others were made in Dholpur and Sikri, after his victory over the Rajputs at nearby Kanwaha.

Nor did the padshah neglect the ceremonial attributes of his new imperial status. According to his daughter, Princess Gulbadan, Babur sent invitations 'in all directions' after his victory at Panipat, so that the Timurid and Chingiz Khanid rulers of Transoxiana could see for themselves the good fortune he enjoyed after 'the Most High had bestowed sovereignty.' His *fathnama* (victory letter), after the defeat inflicted on Rana Sanga was issued on an even more ambitious scale, for it included Shah Tahmasp, the young Persian ruler, as well. Ambassadors from these countries were joined in Agra by 'Hindu envoys', by which Babur presumably meant emissaries of the rulers of Rajasthan.

Another occasion for pomp presented itself at a gathering of Persian and Uzbeg envoys on 18 December 1528. An elaborate ceremony was observed. The padshah was seated in an octagonal pavilion with the Persians on his right and the Uzbegs on his left, high Mughal amirs being deputed to attend to them. Two reverend *khwajas* from Samarqand were assigned places of honour reserved for holy men. 'Before food,' Babur tells us, 'all the sultans, khans, grandees and amirs brought gifts of red, of white, of black (gold, silver and copper coins), of cloth and various other goods.' Never before had such a glittering assembly of dignitaries been seen in Agra, and perhaps not even in Delhi. Silken turbans and gold

27

embroidered *jamahs* of fine muslin and other robes of honour, were presented to the envoys. This represented the practice of gifting 'head to foot' dresses, or *saropa*, to those whom the emperor wished to honour. Exchange of gifts became an established court ceremony throughout Mughal rule.

The guests were also entertained by wrestling matches, fighting elephants and acrobats. Babur was delighted and he described some of these tricks in detail. He had never seen anything like their dizzy gyrations in Central Asia. The festivities reached a climax when 'many dancing girls came also and danced.'

Babur's successors elaborated the court ceremonies on this pattern. They amassed enormous wealth and enjoyed far more opportunities than the dynasty's rugged founder. Protocol became more demanding in the reign of Akbar, the greatest of all the Mughals, who also gave majestic and ample patronage to Hindustani art forms which had appeared only tentatively as entertainment in his grandfather's court.

An Indo-Islamic civilisation, with several distinct cultural manifestations, was already flourishing in Hindustan. The Mughal conquest was followed by an infusion of Persian and Turkish strains which gave new vitality to the Indo-Muslim culture of Hindustan. Nevertheless, Babur longed for the delights of his homeland. He tells us that when one of his emissaries returned from Kabul, 'a melon was brought to me, to cut and eat it affected me strangely: I was all tears!' Indeed, he sent to Balkh for a melon-grower. Before long, he was able to taste the grapes and melons of Central Asia grown in his gardens in Agra.

For sheer amplitude of attainment, there was surely no one in the contemporary world to hold a candle to the extraordinary Turk whose military genius and warmth of personality forever changed the course of Indian history. No finer revelation of the man exists than his fascinating memoirs. He was also a poet of distinction. His end was characteristic. This versatile exemplar of the Eastern renaissance rejected the splendours of Hindustan for a simple gravestone open to the skies of Kabul.

During Humayun's reign the court remained essentially Turkish. The two senior ladies, Babur's widow Maham Begum and his daughter Gulbadan Begum, saw to that. When she was in her sixties, Akbar persuaded his aunt, Gulbadan Begum, to write her memoirs. The old lady is an excellent raconteur. Her *Humayun Nama* artlessly reveals the events of Humayun's downfall, his misadventures in exile and eventual return. She describes two feasts that were celebrated before Humayun lost his throne: the first described as a 'mystic feast' and the other to celebrate her brother Hindal's marriage. A gold embroidered divan was laid in front of the throne on which 'His Majesty and dearest lady sat together.' On this occasion, the lady so honoured was appropriately Khanzada Begum, who had become the senior lady of the family after Maham Begum's death.

The princess' account of the two celebrations staggers the imagination with its lists of jewelled decorations. Central Asian traditions of display combined with the riches of India to create scenes of splendour the likes of which Agra had never seen. There were touches characteristic of Hindustan – the *pan* dishes for instance, betokening the early capitulation of Mughal taste to the pleasures of the betel. But it was essentially a gathering of Central Asian celebrities, including two ladies dressed in men's clothes who were 'adorned by varied accomplishments, such as the making of thumb rings (needed for archery) and arrows, playing polo, and shooting with the bow and arrow. They also played many musical instruments.' Humayun's successors kept bodyguards of these formidable Tartar women.

Though at this time the court was almost wholly foreign in composition and style, it was eclectic in its choice of carpets, European materials — which were already articles of trade — and Indian delicacies. Babur had taken four of Sultan Ibrahim's cooks into his establishment. Epicures are always more catholic in their taste than puritans. Once the process of borrowing started, it was to result in the Indianisation of the Turks, Mongols, Tartars and Persians who sought their fortunes at the imperial court in Agra.

Foreigners no More

During his stay in Persia, Humayun had been drawn to Tabrez by its fame as one of the outstanding centres of urban civilisation in the Islamic world. The celebrated artist, Bihzad, had set up his atelier there, which had become a place of pilgrimage for artists and art lovers. In his straitened circumstances, Humayun could not have impressed anyone, except the most simple, as a likely patron. Nevertheless, he could not resist visiting the atelier. What is more, he seems to have extracted a promise from the artists Mir Sayyid Ali and

Khwaja Abdus Samad to join him when his fortunes improved. When Humayun recovered Kabul, they duly presented themselves at the court in exile.

This turned out to be a momentous decision, for Humayun took lessons from the two masters, and succeeded in persuading his vigorous young son to join him. Almost immediately after they arrived, the two Persian masters were given a major commission. They were to illustrate the Persian Classic *Dastani-i-Amir-Hamzah* in twelve volumes with as many as 1200 paintings. It took them several years to complete and work went on in Agra after Humayun's death, for the artists and their assistants had found a new patron in the young emperor. Only a few of the large paintings on cloth have been preserved, but the great *karkhanah* (atelier) that Akbar established in the fullness of imperial power had its birth in these unobtrusive beginnings.

Though Akbar was averse to the drudgery of studies, he had in full measure the wisdom, judgement and unerring instinct that a tumultuous life imparts. Even in his youth, he was deeply imbued in the temper of the age. If his grandfather was an outstanding paladin of the Oriental renaissance, Akbar was its inheritor. Though formally illiterate, he was sharp and schooled in hardship and a life of action and danger. Such was the young prince who, when not quite fourteen, was crowned padshah in a mango grove near the Himalayan foothills. As the years went by, his concept of kingship was to find expression in the most dazzling court in the age of Oriental splendour.

Akbar spent the first two years of his reign in the Punjab and Delhi. When local resistance had been crushed, in the words of his official biographer Abul Fazl, he 'resolved that the sublime standards should proceed to Agra ... and his ocean-scattering mind decided on travelling by boat on the river Yamuna.' The royal barge was adorned with silks; and when he embarked on 9 October 1558, the amirs followed in a flotilla of decorated boats.

In October when the summer heat had left the plains of Hindustan, the river was quite the most pleasurable way of covering the sixty *kos* (about 200 kilometres) to the capital so precipitately abandoned by Akbar's father. There was no case for haste; the young emperor took three weeks to reach the fort of Badalgarh. The journey was made even more enjoyable by engaging in 'fishing and water-fowling' on the way. We may be sure, too, that Akbar had his barge pull in to the bank whenever he saw a likely landscape, to leap on to a horse and gallop after tigers, nilgai, deer and other game that abounded in the countryside. At night, with the standards furled, the enchanting singers of Hindustan entertained the royal party with music. Bairam Khan had in his entourage the singer Ram Das of Lucknow, who had been one of Salim Shah Sur's musicians. Mulla Abdul Qadir al Badauni, author of *Muntakhab-ut-Tawarikh*, and like Abul Fazl, employed by Akbar, says of Ram Das: 'This man used to be the *Khan-i-Khanan's* companion and intimate associate, and by the beauty of his voice continually brought tears to his eyes.' The melodies would have drifted through the clear night air, borne along by the strains of the *surna* as the *naqqara* responded with the measure of *dhruvapada* in the classical *ragas* of Hindustan.

Akbar had his first view of Agra on 30 October, though

we are not told what he thought of it. Abul Fazl, who was Agra born and a Hindustani at that, became unashamedly lyrical. 'The river Yamuna, which has few like it for the digestibility of its water, flows through it. On either side the amirs erected pleasant homes and made charming gardens which come not within the mould of description. With all grandeur and glory it became once more the abode of the caliphate, and the centre of the sultanate.'

Agra was once again the imperial capital, by virtue of the emperor's presence, and Akbar was the most ambitious and gifted of all the Mughals. With his arrival there, the city's golden age had unquestionably begun.

Akbar, however, was in no hurry to assert himself. Affairs of state were in the trusted hands of Bairam Khan, but a powerful court faction led by the emperor's old chief nurse, Maham Anaga, adopted devious means to undermine the *khan-i-khanan's* position. The real issue was the assertion of Akbar's own authority. By the end of 1562, he had shaken off both. The old warrior met his death at the hands of an assassin with a private grudge while on the way to Mecca, and Maham Anaga's son, Adham Khan, was flung from the ramparts of Badalgarh fort for contriving the murder of the Vizier, Atga Khan.

Akbar was not quite twenty years of age. He was rid of the overbearing pair. At last he was master in his palace and supreme in Hindustan. The year was 1562 and it proved to be a turning point in Mughal rule and the history of India.

The main features of Akbar's policy right up to the end of his long reign in 1605 became clear in the very first decade after 1562, when he took over control of affairs. His immediate objective was to extend the boundaries of the empire and to crush any incipient threat to its security. In a radical break with tradition, he also abolished long-standing measures which discriminated against non-Muslims. With his gift for far-seeing statesmanship, Akbar created institutions designed to give permanence to the empire, a state in which both the ruler and the ruled knew their place. But an institutional framework alone could not give life and soul to the order he visualised. Patronage was extended to the arts, encouragement given to learning and major works undertaken to give expression to the material aspects of civilisation, in the well-understood terms of architectural design, stone and mortar.

From the very beginning, Akbar realised that extension of dominion would be a mirage unless conquest was accompanied by political conciliation. On any reading of the situation, the Rajput princely houses held the key to the security of the empire. Lying directly on his western flank, they could either strengthen it with their support or imperil its very existence. In the past, Muslim invasions had broken on the rocks of fierce Rajput resistance. They were steadfast as friends and unrelenting as foes. Akbar desperately needed them as allies. Accordingly, he set about winning them over by marriage alliances and offers of high-ranking command.

An opportunity for an alliance with the Kachwaha house of Amber presented itself early in 1562. He seized it with undisguised haste. Akbar was on a pilgrimage to the grave in Ajmer of the Chishti mystic, Sheikh Muin-ud-din, when he received Raja Bhara Mal of Amber. What transpired was an offer of marriage with the raja's eldest daughter. The ground must have been carefully prepared in advance. The ceremonies were performed at Sambhar[1] on Akbar's way back from Ajmer.

For the Kachwahas the marriage was a master-stroke. They gained an imperial alliance, and secured for themselves the highest offices in the realm for over a hundred years. The significance for the empire went much deeper. The marriage won the Mughal emperor the support of a powerful Rajput family and was the first positive expression of the secular policies he was to pursue throughout his reign, often in the teeth of fierce orthodox opposition. It was a development without parallel in any contemporary political order.

Akbar further reinforced his policy of conciliation by reversing the long-standing practice of imposing discriminatory taxes on non-Muslims. These had been a regular feature of Muslim rule since the establishment of the Delhi Sultanate at the end of the twelfth century. In 1563, Akbar abolished the vexatious tax on pilgrims visiting Hindu holy places, and followed this the very next year by doing away with the hated *jizya* (poll tax) on non-Muslims. For a young emperor, still finding his way, these measures called for exceptional self-confidence. Binyon has rightly described them as an assertion of Akbar's will and conscience against a tradition sanctioned by centuries of custom.

It could not have been pure coincidence that these immensely significant changes, in what was still essentially an Islamic theocratic state, took place in the two years immediately following Akbar's marriage. It has been customary to give the emperor the entire credit for these epoch-making changes in the character of the regime. There is no question that the *farmans* (edicts) were his, but the Kachwahas must have exploited the leverage they enjoyed. Though the evidence is largely inferential, it is consistent with the influence Akbar's Hindu wives are known to have had on critical occasions. One of those who complained about this influence was Mulla Abdul Qadir al Badauni. He tells us that they urged the emperor to launch a frontal attack on the *Sadr-us-Sudur* (Chief Judge), Sheikh Abdunnabi, and other orthodox divines, for the execution, without his permission, of a Brahmin of Mathura in 1579. Meanwhile, Akbar persisted in his policy of conciliation by *farman* and marriage alliances till, in the last year of the decade, princesses of the ruling houses of Bikaner and Jaisalmer also joined the imperial harem. Ten years later, in his attempt to isolate the Sisodias of Mewar, he contracted a similar alliance with a princess of Dungarpur. Of the leading Rajput houses, Mewar alone stood aloof. Akbar pursued his policy of conciliation and resorted to arms only when other measures had failed, right up to his last years. Mewar defied him to the end, and Rani Durgawati of Gondwana stabbed herself rather than submit.

Akbar took to the field himself to crush a rebellion in Gujarat that threatened the western seaboard of his empire. Mounted on camel-back, in nine days he covered the 730 kilometres to the gates of Ahmedabad. He charged the enemy at the head of a small force as cries of 'Allahu-Akbar' and 'Ya Muin' rent the air. In the fierce battle that followed, Akbar had many a brush with death and saw some of his trusted warriors fall at his side. The fame of this exploit electrified Hindustan and was still being extolled, in bardic lore, fifty years later when foreign travellers had become a common sight at the court of his son, Jahangir.

With the conquest of Kashmir in 1586, the whole of the north, from Kabul to as far south as Khandesh, and from Gujarat in the west to Bengal in the east, had been incorporated in Akbar's empire. Sind and Orissa were added in 1593. All that was left to make his the first truly Indian Muslim empire was the annexation of the three Deccan kingdoms of Ahmednagar, Bijapur and Golconda. In the last years of the century, his half-hearted sons and a succession of self-seeking amirs were entrusted with the Deccan campaign. It was soon bogged down in suspicion, intrigues and ineffectual action in the field. Now sixty years of age, the emperor put himself in command. Ahmednagar fell on 28 August 1600, and Asirgarh in January 1601, though not before his officers had bribed the garrison. At this point the campaign had to be called off abruptly, because Prince Salim's incipient rebellion demanded the emperor's presence at the power centre in Agra.

As a conqueror, Akbar fell somewhat short of his two ancestors, Chingiz Khan and Timur. They conquered half of the Euro-Asian landmass and laid it to waste. Timur, it is true, built peerless monuments in Samarqand, and in the tradition of the Turks framed institutes of government; but the hearts of men of the armies of these two conquerors smote turned cold at the mere mention of their names. In the creative genius of empire building, both fell far short of their descendant's

37

achievements in India. And in magnanimity and personal bravery Akbar set an example far beyond the heroes of the age.

All honour is due to the gallant defenders of Chitor, Rana Pratap of Mewar and the heroic Rani Durgawati of Gondwana, who preferred death to what she saw as dishonour. In the last analysis, however, the unification of the country was a higher aim. The Mughals were strangers no more.

Orders, Spiritual and Temporal

Within three years of initiating his whirlwind career of conquest, there was no longer any doubt about Akbar's pre-eminence in Hindustan. The emperor had evidently been thinking of giving some tangible expression to the prestige of his regime. This is how Abul Fazl puts it: 'Accordingly, he at this time (1565) gave directions for the building in Agra — which by its position is the centre of Hindustan — of a grand fortress such as might be worthy thereof, and correspond to the dignity of his dominions.' The 'grand fortress' that stands there today was 'completed with all its battlements, breastwork, and its loop-holes, in the space of eight years, under the faithful superintendence of Qasim Khan, Mir Barr-u-Bahr.'[2] An auspicious time for commencement of work was assigned by astrologers.

Work proceeded apace. According to Akbar's biographer, the emperor built as many as five hundred palaces, pavilions and residences within the ample walls of the fort in Bengali, Gujarati and other indigenous styles. Even in his early years Akbar had established a considerable court. All the imperial offices, ladies of the royal household and harem, key officials, court servants and guards had to be accommodated. The Rajput queen from Amber was able to occupy Bengali Mahal in 1569. However, the court was not destined to stay in Agra fort much longer. Though children had been born to some of the emperor's wives, none had survived. Greatly troubled, Akbar sought the intercession of the saint of Sikri, Sheikh Salim Chishti. The hermit's blessings were reputed to work miracles. Akbar revealed to him the cause of his distress, and the saint consoled him with a promise of not one but three sons.

The Rajput queen duly became enceinte. A small palace was made for her in the shadow of the saint's hermitage while the emperor himself, in accordance with Turkish custom, stayed behind in Agra. There was great rejoicing when news of the birth of a son was brought to him, and the young prince was named Salim in honour of the saint. Murad and Daniyal were born to ladies of the harem in quick succession. Akbar was thus assured of an heir.

Akbar had made a vow that, if, blessed with a son, as an act of thanksgiving he would walk to the shrine of Khwaja Muin-ud-din Chishti in Ajmer and 'day devotion to God.' Accordingly, he set out on 20 January 1570, covering the distance of 364 kilometres in 16 days. Akbar once walked the 48.28 kilometres from Mathura to Agra so fast that only three of his entourage could keep pace with him. This time, however, it was a pilgrimage and not a test of physical endurance. He spent several days in devotion at the shrine and distributed gifts. From Ajmer he went on to the shrines of

Nizam-ud-din Auliya and other saints in Delhi before returning to Agra.

Two years later his gratitude was expressed in the foundation of a capital on the saint's hill. It was in this capital, renamed Fatehpur, after Akbar's victory in Gujarat, that the emperor created temporal and spiritual institutions for the governance and good order of his empire. The developments that followed profoundly influenced the destiny of the Mughal empire, and more remotely the country as well but they will be described here only to the extent that they affected the minds and lives of the court in Agra.

The most ambitious of the young emperor's projects was the attempt to establish an over-arching social order in which, in the words of his son Jahangir, 'the road to altercation would be closed.' The historian Asaf Khan said of Akbar, 'His heart is inclined to justice, desiring that the followers of different faiths, each having become acquainted with the truth of the others' religion, should act with restraint and abandon bigotry.' After he moved the court to Fatehpur Sikri, the great question on which Akbar initiated debate was: 'If some true knowledge was ... everywhere to be found, why should truth be confined to one religion?' He went on to enunciate the principle of *Sulh Kul* (Universal Concord). He had already abolished discriminatory taxes. Had Akbar stopped there, he would have been remembered as a true eclectic, who made a courageous attempt to establish a reign of tolerance as the social and religious counterpart of the political unity of his varied dominions.

The practical question, however, was how to get away from the rigid confines of orthodoxy. Akbar's coadjutors were the pliable trio, Sheikh Mubarak and his two sons, Faizi and Abul Fazl. Along with some other rationalists, they evolved a theory of the emperor's supreme authority to determine religious disputes. A *Mazhar Nama* (declaration) to this effect was adopted by the principal *ulama* in 1579. But secularism as a guiding principle of state policy was unknown in those times. There had to be a set of beliefs and practices to which people could adhere. Accordingly, an ill-assorted jumble was devised which in time came to be called *Din Ilahi*, or Divine Faith. Nothing loathe, Akbar went even further and adopted an elaborate ceremonial for the admission of disciples. The central purpose of these measures was to transcend the differences of established religions and to draw the people together in allegiance to the emperor himself. The new faith, however, was totally devoid of any metaphysic or abiding appeal, it only managed to confuse and perplex court circles. The daring attempt to institutionalise the semi-divinity of the emperor was misconceived. Though shaken, orthodoxy held fast to its moorings.

Badauni, a hostile critic, puts it like this: 'At a council meeting for renovation of the religion of the empire, Raja Bhagwan (Das) said, "I would willingly believe that Hindus and Musalmans have each a bad religion; but only tell me where the new sect is, and what opinion they hold, so that I may believe." His Majesty reflected a little, and ceased to urge the Raja.' Clearly Akbar was at a loss. He had even less success with his outstanding general, Raja Man Singh.

Din Ilahi won only one Hindu adherent at court, Akbar's boon companion, Birbal. Some Muslim officials became

41

disciples. On the vast mass of his subjects, Akbar's new faith made no impact at all. It did not long survive his death, but its grand design of universal concord has a powerful message for all time. In the last analysis, Raja Bhagwan Das and Mulla Abdul Qadir al Badauni rather than Abul Fazal Allami were the representative voices of the age.

Akbar's pious hope that all men should subscribe to a universal social order was a magnificent failure. Not so his resolve to create a political order in which men knew with reasonable certainty the obligations of status. This, in contrast, was a glorious success.

Initially, the authority of the empire had no sanction other than successful conquest, and this authority was embodied in the *shahinshah* himself. Even before Akbar died, however, a profound change was becoming apparent in the substance of authority. The right to rule was recognised to be derived from legitimacy rather than conquest. This development was unquestionably Akbar's most important contribution to the country's history. So compelling became the mystique of Mughal supremacy that neither the Marathas nor the British, the two strongest contenders for the succession to power, could bring themselves to question it. The magic of its name outlived the substance of actual power by a hundred years. The aura was essentially Akbar's creation.

The system of government was interlocked with a ranking order called *mansabdari*. A *mansab* was a grant of land coupled with the requirement to muster a specified number of mounted and foot soldiers. Superficially, it resembled the feudal system, with the important difference being that the *mansabdars* were essentially imperial appointees. Grants were not hereditary, being subject to resumption on death. This had important consequences both for the grantees and the ryots. The former had no interest in their *mansabs* beyond squeezing them to the limits of endurance. Correspondingly, the ryots saw no earthly use in developing their land, when the only prospect in sight was being relieved of more if they produced more. Unquestionably, this is the origin of mass rural poverty.

With Akbar atop this administrative pyramid, the vast army of officials were kept on their toes. The bonds loosened during succeeding reigns. According to early foreign travellers, lawlessness became rampant under Jahangir, sweeping up to the very gates of Agra. An imperial system necessarily took colour from the personality of the emperor. None of Akbar's successors possessed anything like his genius for combining firmness with conciliation, and of extracting work from his prodigious army of officials because he never spared himself.

The Power and the Glory

Early in his reign, Akbar's subjects must have been a little nonplussed by their unusual emperor. As he galloped after game through the countryside, or listened to enchanting ditties in praise of Sheikh Muin-ud-din Chishti, or charged elephants in combat, or took delight in the strange game of polo in the ground alongside the old fort of Badalgarh, he might have seemed someone whose 'collar they could touch.' Seated in the Diwan-i-am of his massive new Agra fort he was a different being altogether. Here was all the power and glory of an empire greater than any seen since the days of Ashoka and

Chandragupta. For here he was the *shahinshah*, the embodiment of all authority in matters of the state. With the issue of the *Mazhar Nama* in 1579, he became also the Imam of the age. The *shahinshah* was thus the vice-regent of God, clothed with temporal and spiritual authority undreamt of in the contemporary world.

Abul Fazl tells us that the fort was manned on all four sides by guards of nobles, *ahadis* and other troops. Akbar was protected by a personal bodyguard of twenty chosen warriors. 'The inside of the harem is guarded by sober and active women, the most trustworthy of them are placed about the apartments of His Majesty. Outside the enclosure the eunuchs are placed and, at a proper distance, there is a guard of faithful Rajputs, beyond whom are the porters of the gates.'

The women, who are disarmingly described as 'sober and active,' were Tartars armed with bows and arrows and short daggers. They were called *Urdu Begis*, which may be loosely rendered as Regiment of Honourable Women. These formidable palace guards were far from being purely ornamental, as Prince Salim learnt to his cost while he was still heir apparent. He had seized a madman who had strayed into the private apartments, and was so set upon by the amazons that Akbar had to drag him out of their clutches by the hair.

The security of the emperor depended in the last resort on the 'faithful Rajputs.' At Chitor and Ranthambhor they had held out against Akbar's forces before throwing themselves at the siege guns. These were the men to whose courage and loyalty Akbar entrusted the inviolability of his person, whether in Agra fort or anywhere else in the empire.

44

Akbar's public ceremonies were coloured by a heterodox mixture of Hindu and Parsi rites. After performing his morning devotions, the first thing he did was to step out into the balcony to greet the rising sun, glistening with the colours of dawn the great river Yamuna flowing away eastwards. Here, says Abul Fazl, 'he is visible ... to people of all ranks ... without any molestation from the macebearers. This mode of showing himself is called, in the language of the country, *darshan*.' It was, of course, an old Hindu custom, which Akbar adopted as a living compact with the citizens of Agra and, through them, with the people of his empire. The *darshaniyas*, as they were called, virtually became a cult group, and the practice continued in succeeding reigns.

After the first watch, about nine o'clock in the morning, it was time for the emperor's next *darshan*. This was a formal occasion when he appeared in his *jharoka* (audience balcony) facing the Diwan-i-am. An audience was sometimes also arranged in the evening or at night. Not even personal tragedy prevented Akbar from performing his part. When the Queen Mother, Mariam Makani, died on 20 August 1604, the author who completed the *Akbar Nama* says, 'Who shall describe the grief of His Majesty? He shaved his hair, moustaches, etc. and cast off his turban and donned the garb of woe. He was the first to bear the body on his shoulder, and then the grandees conveyed it in turn.' In conformity with the edicts of Chingiz Khan, he even shaved his eyebrows. The very next day he sat in the *jharoka* to receive the public's salutations and ordered the celebration of Dussehra, the principal Hindu festival, in all its ceremonial. To the end Akbar put duty before all else.

When the emperor held court, says Abul Fazl, 'they beat a large drum.' The drumming of ten pairs of *damana* (large kettle drums), from the roof of the *naqqar khana* (Drum House) near Hathi Pol gate, set up a formidable reverberation which could have been heard far out in the city. All those who had business, and many who did not, but could not endure the thought of not being seen, hurried to the gates on horse-back, in palanquins or on foot. Attendance at the morning audience in the Diwan-i-am was obligatory for the higher ranking dignitaries. Bernier tells us that his Agha, Danishmand Khan, enjoyed exemption because of his distinguished position at court, but usually attended nevertheless.

Protocol inside the palace was regulated to the minutest detail. 'His Majesty's sons and grandchildren, the grandees of the court, and all other men who have admittance, attend to make the *komish*, and remain standing in their proper places according to their rank.' The *komish* was the salutation prescribed for regular attendants. It was devised by the emperor himself. 'One day,' Akbar recalled, 'my royal father bestowed on me one of his own caps, which I put on. Because the cap of the king was rather large, I had to hold it with my (right) hand whilst holding my head downwards.' Humayun professed to be so pleased that from the feeling of propriety, ordered this to be the mode of *kornish* and *taslim*. The latter, says Abul Fazl, 'consists in placing the back of the right hand on the ground, and then raising it gently till the person stands erect, when he puts the palm of his hand upon the crown of his head, which pleasing manner of saluting signifies that he is ready to give himself as an offering.'

For most normal darbars, the *kornish* was appropriate. More elaborate modes were prescribed for special occasions. We are told that upon taking leave, or presentation, or receiving a *mansab*, a *jagir*, or dress of honour, or an elephant, or a horse, the rule was to make three *taslims*; but only one on all other occasions, when salaries were paid, or gifts presented to those whom the emperor wished to honour.

Akbar did not stop short at these customary salutations. He audaciously claimed the right to prostration, or *sijda*, which is one of the positions at prayer, and therefore looked upon as the exclusive prerogative of God. Abul Fazl was ingenious enough to find a justification even for this sacrilege. For disciples of Akbar's *Din-i-Ilahi*, 'it was necessary to add something ... and they look upon a prostration before his Majesty as a prostration before God, for royalty is an emblem of the power of God, and a light-shedding ray from this Sun of the Absolute.'

Akbar surrounded himself at all times of the day with crowds of people. He was accessible. Justice and public audience were his two principal instruments for satisfying the expectations of his subjects, and he arranged his daily programme so that he could regularly perform the duties of a sovereign.

The example he set, in form at least, was religiously followed by his successors. Personal variations were introduced. Jahangir installed what he picturesquely called the chain of justice. 'After my accession, the first order that I gave was for the fastening up of the chain of justice, so that if those engaged in the administration of justice should delay or practise hypocrisy, the oppressed might come to this chain and shake it so that its noise might attract attention.' It was made of four maunds of pure gold, was thirty yards long and strung with sixty bells. One end was secured to the battlements of Shah Burj, the emperor's pavilion, and the other to a stone post on the river bank, where it was accessible to all who passed. Numerous instances are known of Jahangir's obsession with the administration of justice. The chain may not have been pulled very often or energetically enough to attract the emperor's attention, but its presence was an assurance to all men. Shah Jahan did away with the *sijda*, though in his anxiety to live up to Akbar's demanding standards, he seems to have done with just two *pahars* of sleep.[3]

Life and Times

Crowned when he was barely fourteen, Akbar made the most of his salad years, before the climatic events of 1562 led to his taking over personal control of the affairs of state. While he was still in Delhi, he seems to have been fascinated by the Indian elephant. By the time he was sixteen, he had gained complete mastery over this ponderous yet strangely sage animal. The Turk in him demanded conflict. He learned to dominate even *mast* elephants. His son Jahangir records that he was often seen to leap on the backs of these dangerous animals from a wall or overhanging branch and subdue them.

One of his most stirring encounters was seen by thousands of wonder-struck citizens of his new capital of Agra. Akbar picked on Hawai (like the wind), a beast that had been Himu's mount at the Battle of Panipat. 'In choler, passionateness,

fierceness and wickedness,' says Abul Fazl, 'he was a match for
the world,' and his opponent, Ranbagha, was nearly as
formidable. Akbar, who later admitted to Salim that he had
taken two or three cups of wine, was in high spirits. He chased
Ranbagha to the boat bridge, and when his adversary
mounted, Akbar put Hawai on his tracks. 'At each step,'
Akbar confessed to his son, 'came the thought that the lashings
might give way. People seeing this were overwhelmed in the
sea of perplexity and alarm. As the care and guardianship of
the Great and Glorious God is ever and in all places the
protection of this humble suppliant, both elephants crossed
the bridge in safety.' Once over, Ranbagha made off as fast as
he could.

If elephants were a novelty, polo was in his blood. One of
the first things Akbar did after his ceremonial arrival in Agra
was to lay a polo ground alongside the old fort of Badalgarh.
His *begs* were press-ganged into hectic games on the dusty strip
between the fort and river. It was a game that the incredulous
populace of Agra had never seen. They had been accustomed
to the more stately comings and goings of the Hindustani
sultans of the past. Who was this ferocious Central Asian,
spurring his Turki horse, and flailing away with a hooked stick
at a wooden ball darting between the flashing hooves? A
variation that the inventive mind of the emperor introduced
was the night game with burning balls of palas wood.[4] A
favourite resort for this sport was Nagarchain (Place of
Repose), a few miles south of the capital.

Hunting was as much in Akbar's Turkish blood as polo.
The *qamargah*, or encirclement of game with a closing ring of

horses, was a standard manoeuvre. In his early years the craving for danger demanded close personal encounters. There was time enough for *qamargahs* when he had had his fill. Hindustan was teeming with game of all kinds. One of his most celebrated encounters was with a tigress with five cubs near the fort of Narwar, while he was on the way back from his lightning conquest of Malwa. Akbar was just nineteen and in his prime. 'His Majesty,' says Abul Fazl, 'with swift foot and alert arm attacked the brute and killed it by one stroke of his sword.'

Akbar's skill and courage must have been phenomenal. It is inconceivable that a tigress with five cubs did not fight savagely before succumbing to a single blow of his sword.

The young Prince Salim, who took to shooting from the age of twelve, was brought up on the weapons fashioned by Akbar's *ustads*. His maximum bag in one day was eighteen deer. Jahangir remained essentially a connoisseur. He was no wanton slaughterer of tigers. The total of eighty-six he notched up would have seemed juvenile to our former 'sporting' maharajas, one of whom claimed that his count was heading for 1300 before he quit.

Jahangir freely gave the palm for shooting to the Empress Nur Jahan. While the camp was at Ajmer, she shot four tigers with six shots. Jahangir declared: 'Until now such shooting was never seen, that from top of an elephant and inside of a howdah six shots should be made and not one missed.'

Before Nur Jahan joined Jahangir's harem, her first husband, Sher Afghan (tiger-killer) had been killed in suspicious circumstances. A wag promptly recited the following lines:

Though Nur Jahan be in form a woman
In the ranks of men she's a tiger-slayer.

Nur Jahan made quite as complete a conquest of her royal husband. The historian Mutamad Khan complains that 'the emperor granted Nur Jahan the rights of sovereignty and government ... Coin was struck in her name, with the superscription: "By the order of the King Jahangir, gold has a hundred splendours added to it by receiving the impression of the name of Nur Jahan, the Queen Begum."' Jahangir virtually abdicated to her, and things 'reached such a pass that the king was such only in name. Repeatedly he asserted that he had bestowed the sovereignty on Nur Jahan Begum, and would say, "I require nothing beyond a *ser* of wine and half a *ser* of meat."'

Even before Jahangir capitulated to his Persian beauty, the ladies of the harem were very far from being mere residents subject to the emperor's whims. The senior ladies, and particularly such dowagers and elderly aunts as Mariam Makani and Gulbadan Begum, enjoyed an authority on tradition and etiquette that was virtually supreme. Their control over the channels of communication within the palace – the eunuchs and serving girls who carried messages, overheard conversations and dusted the poison of gossip on the intricate web of internal relations, was such that many a court intrigue could be traced to them.

Akbar himself, whether from policy or genuine conjugality, was influenced by the Rajput queen, who after the birth of Salim, was renamed Mariam Zamani. Mulla Abdul Qadir al Badauni attributed Akbar's celebration of the Hindu rite of *havan* to his 'affection towards the Hindu princesses of his harem.' In his peevish way Badauni complained that they 'had gained so great an ascendancy over him as to make him forswear beef, garlic, onions and the wearing of a beard ...'

After he had killed Dara Shikoh, even the smug puritan Aurangzeb pursued his brother's favourite concubine, Ranadil (Clear Heart), with his unwelcome attentions. She gashed her face with a dagger to mar her beauty so that the emperor would leave her in peace. Aurangzeb's grandson, Jahandar Shah, openly sported with the notorious concubine, Lal Kunwar, who claimed descent from Akbar's master of music, Tan Sen; but that was in the days of the empire's political and moral decline.

Because of the excesses that disfigured court life in the long years of decline, the cultural function of the harem is often overlooked. The graces of conversation and good manners were perfected in the elegant environment of the private apartments, and the harem also had an important role in the cultural education of children of the royal blood.

The emperor's harem, consisting of his wives and concubines, was a very exclusive establishment. Most of Akbar's alliances were of a political character, aimed at gaining the good will of powerful families. According to Monserrate, there were as many as three hundred ladies in Akbar's seraglio. Abul Fazl tells us that admission was eagerly sought by ladies of the amirs. Requests were scrutinised with great care, and aspirants who were not permanently admitted were allowed to stay for a month at a time.

The women of the palace were far more numerous and in a different class altogether. Akbar had more than five thousand, and each one was given a separate apartment. These women were the entertainers, the singers and dancers who embellished the arts of song and dance to a degree never before attained. Francois Bernier, the French physician in Danishmand Khan's service, was much taken by their skill as dancers. 'Most of these *kanchanis* are handsome and well-dressed and sing to perfection; and their limbs being extremely supple, they dance with wonderful agility, and are always correct in regard to time.' Bernard, a Frenchman at Jahangir's court, was so taken by a *kanchani* during a performance that he demanded her hand. Jahangir was delighted. Bernard was allowed to carry away his lady love on his shoulders and later he married her.

What proved more enduring in the cultural field had its origin in the commission given by Humayun to the two Persian artists who joined him from Tabrez, to paint more than a thousand folios to illustrate the Persian epic, *Dastan-i-Amir Hamzah*. Humayun's sudden death might have terminated this stupendous undertaking had the young Akbar not urged them on. Consequently, the two artists, Abdus Samad and Mir Sayyid Ali, were obliged to set up an atelier in Agra to complete the task. Painters joined them from wherever they could be found, though principally from Gujarat in the west and later, after Kashmir was annexed in 1586, from there too. Indigenous painters could draw on centuries of continuous experience. Traditional themes were being executed with vibrant artistic feeling and a strong sense of colour. Akbar's *karkhanah* had no difficulty in attracting recruits with established reputations for distinction in the art of painting.

Akbar himself 'discovered' Daswant, whose unlikely traditional occupation was that of palanquin bearer. 'In a short time', says Abul Fazl, 'he surpassed all painters, and became the first master of the age.' Basawan, too, excelled in backgrounding, drawing of features, distribution of colours and portrait painting. These specialisations reveal the manner in which the imperial *karkhanah* functioned. Most miniatures, particularly in the Akbari period, were the work of two or more painters – one doing the outline, another the portraits and often a third the colouring. Attributions were given in colophons.

Under Akbar the painters were directly involved in the contemporary events they painted. For example, when Akbar made his historic dash in 1572 across the desert to crush the rebellion in Gujarat, no less than three painters were included in the picked band of twenty-seven who accompanied him ahead of the main force. They were Jagannath, Sanwal Das and Tara Chand. Historical or legendary events must have been very vividly described to the artists because their miniatures in the large number of works commissioned are exceedingly animated and colourful. That they were executed by masters is evident from the miniatures in public and private collections all over the world. More than a hundred painters 'have become famous masters of the art,' Abul Fazl declares, 'whilst the number of those who approach perfection ... is very large.' It should come as no surprise that 'this is especially true of the Hindus; their pictures surpass our conception of things. Few, indeed, in the whole world are found to equal them.' The remarkably vigorous school had clearly reached maturity.

Equally significant was the mastery of Persian models and techniques achieved by the highly adaptable Indian artists. The number of *ustads* of foreign origin diminished progressively, until, in Shah Jahan's reign, Abul Hassan Nadir-uz-Zaman (Wonder of the Age) was probably the only one left.

The most prolific period followed Akbar's establishment of the Agra *karkhanah*. Commissions were given in rapid succession. The *Chingiz Nama, Zafar Nama* (History of the House of Timur), his own *Akbar Nama*, and the classical Sanskrit works of India such as the *Ramayana* and the *Mahabharata*, which the emperor had translated into Persian.

Jahangir's interest was more aesthetic than historical. During his reign the individual artist often worked on his own, and favoured subjects were flowers, birds and animals. Mansur's work was distinguished by meticulous attention to detail though without any loss of animation. Portraits continued to attract great attention. Nothing pleased the Mughal emperors more than flattering portraits of themselves. Jahangir fancied himself with a halo and his feet firmly planted on a sphere representing the world. He claimed to be able to identify the work of individual artists, even to the extent of perceiving 'Whose work the original face is, and who has painted the eyes and eyebrow.' Shah Jahan's head artist was the Hindustani Muslim Faqirullah Khan, and Dara Shikoh, his eldest son, was a celebrated patron. Even Aurangzeb, though generally unfavourable to the arts, took keen pleasure in flattering portraits of himself. But his reputation was enough to scatter artists of the famed imperial *karkhanah* to other courts and patrons, thus stimulating the growth of lively local and regional schools in the eighteenth and early nineteenth centuries.

There was a parallel development in music, which was almost wholly indigenous in structure, melodic interpretation and feeling. The patronage given by Bairam Khan and Akbar has already been mentioned. Music continued to flourish until Aurangzeb banished it from the court. About a thousand performers, who were unable to adjust themselves immediately to the deprivation of an imperial patron, staged a mock burial of music. Aurangzeb was attracted by the sound of wailing to the walls of his palace in Delhi. When told what it was all about he remarked acidly that the 'body' should be buried so deep that its voice would never again be heard. The deathblow was not complete. Music survived in the mahals of the amirs. As had happened with painting, the performers also spread out all over Hindustan in search of patrons, giving rise to flourishing *gharanas* that survive to this day.

City of Spectacles

Once the capital of a struggling sultanate, the Mughals had made Agra the seat of the greatest empire seen in Hindustan for a thousand years. It became a kaleidoscope of colour and brilliant spectacles.

One of Akbar's innovations was the revival of the old Hindu custom of the sovereign's ceremonial weighing against articles of value. What made it specially noteworthy was that the ceremony was observed by a Muslim ruler of a dynasty only recently arrived in Hindustan. After his introduction of the

Divine Era dating from his accession, Akbar was ceremonially weighed twice a year on both his solar and lunar birthdays.

The harem had an important function in these ceremonies. In Akbar's reign his mother Mariam Makani presided over arrangements. When the day arrived, a long string preserved in the harem was solemnly knotted. This is the origin of the word *salgirah* (birthday knot), which has become the accepted current word for birthday. The articles to be weighed were sent by the ladies of the royal household. On the solar birthday the emperor was weighed against each of twelve articles starting with the costliest, among them gold, quicksilver, silk, perfumes, copper, ghee, iron, rice and milk. The lunar birthday weighing was against eight articles, of which silver and tin were the most expensive. Later, the value of the articles weighed was distributed to mendicants and poor people crowding the palace. Since promotions and rewards were announced and costly gifts presented, the emperor's birthdays were eagerly awaited by the hordes of courtiers thronging the capital.

The most colourful of the festivals celebrated by Akbar was the old Parsi feast of *Nauroz* (New Year). It commenced on the day when the sun moved into Aries, and lasted till the nineteenth day. Two days were specially auspicious, when money and presents were given away. Banquets were held and drums were beaten to mark each *pahar*, and to announce the arrival of singers and musicians.

Akbar believed that fire and light were manifestations of the divine, and that it was a religious duty to worship them. Every year, at noon of the day when the sun entered the nineteenth degree of Aries, a fire was lit by exposing a *surajkrant*[5] to the rays of the sun. The fire was carefully tended the whole year, until the ceremony was performed all over again. At sunset, twelve candles in gold and silver stands were lit and brought before the emperor, while a singer, with a candle in his hand, sang praises to God and invoked His blessings for the continuance of the reign. Akbar himself designed one of the candle stands, and some of the candles were so tall that ladders had to be used to snuff them.

Akbar borrowed freely from Hindu and Parsi practices to create a ritual of his own to go with his new faith. For example, tall metal lamps, with tiers of oil wicks, are commonly used in Hindu temples, and the fire pot was taken from the Parsis. A large lantern, called *akash diya* (sky lamp), was suspended from the top of a pole no less than forty Akbari yards high, supported by sixteen ropes, in front of the Diwan-i-am. The *akash diya* signified that the light of the king's majesty shone over the realm.

Yet another festive occasion was the *Khushroz* (Joyful Day), on the third feast day of every month. Stalls were arranged just beyond the Diwan-i-am in Agra fort where 'people of His Majesty's harem come, and the women of other men also are invited, and buying and selling is quite general.' Badauni tells us, with a perceptible dash of venom, that Akbar decided to open the stalls for some time, 'for the enjoyment of the Begums and the women of the harem, and also for any other married ladies. On such occasions, His Majesty spent much money, and the important affairs of the harem people, marriage contracts, and betrothals of boys and girls, were arranged at such meetings.'

An unstated purpose of the monthly *mina bazaar* was to give the ladies of the amirs an opportunity to vie with each other in attracting the emperor's attention. It is quite out of character that Akbar left it to his palace chamberlain to recruit women to his enormous harem. What better occasion than the fancy fair for the emperor to spot them himself? It became a kind of monthly Royal Ascot at which the most highly bred, beautiful and talented ladies of the realm freely displayed their charms. Salim was ensnared by the lady who eventually became Empress, Nur Jahan at just such a fair. Shah Jahan, Manucci declares, perambulated through the crowds in his palanquin, indicating to his attendants which of the women should be conducted to his harem. Akbar had five thousand of them, and Jahangir six, but Shah Jahan was much more modest with only two.

As may be expected, Abul Fazl imputed a higher purpose to the emperor; he took advantage of the *mina bazaar* to find out for himself the state of trade and prices of articles. He claims, too, that people laid their grievances before him, 'without being prevented by the mace-bearers.' *Khushroz* thus became an occasion for interchange between the palace and the people. Young bucks and aspiring debutantes could display their finery and indulge in licenced flirtation, while the ladies satisfied their fancy for trinkets and the foreign trifles that had begun to find their way to the city of the Great Mughal by sea and the overland trade routes.

If Akbar was concerned with symbolic meanings, his down-to-earth grandson, Shah Jahan, was frankly obsessed with display. His sobriquet — the Magnificent — is well merited. In the very first year of his reign he ordered the demolition of the mahals made in Agra fort by Akbar and his own father, sparing only the Jahangiri Mahal. These were replaced by lavishly decorated white marble palaces. Red sandstone was much too drab for him. Nor was he content with the six thrones left by his forbears. A throne of unrivalled magnificence was commissioned, under the superintendence of Bebadal Khan, who was responsible for the goldsmiths' department.

According to Mulla Abdul Lahori, Shah Jahan's official biographer, the emperor had intended to make such use of the enormous imperial treasure 'that beholders might share and benefit by their splendour and that His Majesty might shine with increased brilliancy.' Jewels worth 296 lakh of rupees and one lakh *tolas* of pure gold[6] were made over to Bebadal Khan.

This apparently represents only the cost of materials. According to the *Tarikh-I-Mufazzali*, the throne was completed at a cost of nine crores, nine lakhs and one thousand rupees. Tavernier was informed that the cost was 10.70 crores. Whatever the cost may have been, it is obvious that Shah Jahan intended the throne to be far more magnificent than anything conceived so far.

According to the *Shah Nama* of Inayat Khan, the throne took seven years to be made and Shah Jahan took his seat on it on *Id-i-Fitr*, during the *Nauroz* of AH 1044 (equivalent to 1634-35) on his return from the Deccan. Among the precious stones set in the throne was a ruby presented by Shah Abbas Safavi of Persia to Jahangir, on which were inscribed the names of his ancestors up to Timur.

The finished throne was not as grand as the specifications given to Bebadal Khan. On the top of each pillar there were to be two peacocks, 'thickset with gems.' Tavernier examined it with the appraising eye of a jeweller after it had been shifted along with the court to Delhi. It was smaller and indeed far finer. The seat rested on massive gold, gem-encrusted feet, and was covered with a canopy supported by twelve columns on three side, the front being open to the court. The canopy was studded with gems and set off by a fringe of pearls. On top was 'a peacock with (an) elevated tail made of blue sapphires and other coloured stones, the body of gold with inlaid precious stones having a large ruby in front of the breast, whence hangs a pearshaped pearl of 50 carats or thereabouts. On both sides ... there is a large bouquet of the same height as the bird, consisting of many kinds of flowers, made of gold inlaid with precious stones.'

Tavernier counted as many as 108 of the finest rubies, some of 200 carats or more, and 116 emeralds. 'In my opinion,' says Tavernier, 'the most costly point about this magnificent throne is that the twelve columns supporting the canopy are surrounded by beautiful rows of pearls, which are round and of fine water.' The throne was flanked by two *chhattris* of ornately embroidered red velvet, one on either side, with long, bejewelled handles. For fear of tiring his readers, Tavernier sensibly refrained from describing the gems in five other gold and silver thrones placed in an apartment nearby.

When Nadir Shah sacked Delhi in 1739, the Peacock Throne was his most prized trophy. It was subsequently broken up in the dynastic confusion in Persia. Pieces were retrieved which later were assembled in the form of a more conventional seat. The fabulous Peacock Throne became a memory even before the House of Timur for whose emperors it was seven years in the making.

Objective descriptions of the sights and sounds of the capital appear only incidentally in the chronicles. The weighing ceremonies, for instance, come to life not in Abul Fazl's pages but in the miniatures of Akbar's artists. Less concerned with the deeper significance of royalty, some foreign visitors to the court of the Great Mughal have left graphic accounts of what they actually saw.

Few accounts of the Mughal capital are more lively than the *Relations* of Peter Mundy. This mercurial Cornishman spent some years at the English factory in *mohalla* Phulhatti, and revelled in the excitement of life in the city during Shah Jahan's reign. Dressed as a Hindustani, after the prevailing fashion of English factors in those early days, Mundy was able to freely mix with the people and take in the scene. To cap it all, he was adept at making quick sketches which admirably illustrate his graphic account of this age of magnificence.

On 1 June 1632, the city was astir in the early hours. Shah Jahan was expected on his return from the Deccan. Mundy forged his way through the crowds with his interpreter Sundar Das. Ahead of the main column, they came upon camels with panniers carrying men and women servants, a multitude of baggage elephants and camels, and then over 160 elephants carrying covered *ambaris* (howdahs) in all colours, each with at least four of the emperor's women and those of the amirs accompanying him. Thousands of horsemen with long lances glittering in the sun were careering over the plain. 'All the face of the earth, soe far as wee could see, was covered with people, troopes of horse, eliphants etts, with innumerable flaggs small and greate, which made a most gallant show.'

Saif Khan's wife, who was a sister of the emperor's late wife, Mumtaz Mahal, travelled in great state, in a *chandauli* (palanquin suspended between two elephants), cooled by fragrant screens of khas roots. There were twenty coaches for the emperor and about twenty elephants, covered with gold embroidered trappings and carrying the kings arms, 'which is a tiger couchant with the sun rising over his back ... Then came the king himself mounted on a dark grey horse, and with him Mahabat Khan,' followed by prince Dara Shikoh, and behind him all the amirs. 'All these moving in on one, on so many huge elephants, seemed like a fleet of ships with flags and streamers ... so that all these together made a most majestical, war-like and delightsome sight.'

The great cavalcade halted at Dera ka Bagh for the emperor to dismount. There he remained till the tenth of the month. Then, at midnight, Shah Jahan made for the citadel of Agra in a closed palanquin, the date and time being determined by astrologers.

Only nine days later, Mundy joined crowds in the street to watch Shah Jahan's progress to the Idgah for *Id-ul-Zuha* prayers. The emperor was seated in a gorgeous *ambari* atop his father's favourite elephant. 'As he passed, he flung gold among the people.' Custom prescribed that when the emperor was mounted on horseback, the amirs walked behind; but when on an elephant, they were permitted the liberty of riding horses, and the really great ones on elephants, in the rear. Shah Jahan's ensigns were held aloft, twelve copper *damanas* (large drums) were beaten slowly together, while eight feet long trumpets made a 'base, hollow sound, neither rising nor falling.'

Not even Mundy could have asked for more, but be had to wait only six months for the most spectacular display of the age of magnificence. In February 1633, the two princes Dara Shikoh and Shuja were married. Mundy was not invited to the marriage feasts and other celebrations inside the palace; but, like the populace, he was free to watch such a display of fireworks as had never before been seen. They were let off in the strand below the fort, where animal fights had been arranged for the emperor's father. Mundy describes 'great elephants whose bellies were full of squibbs, crackers etc; giants with wheels in their hands, then a rank of monsters, then of turrets, then of artificial trees (and other) inventions, all full of rockets etc, as was the rail round about. All these being fired, although not at one time, innumerable were the rockets, reports, squibbs and crackers that flew about and aloft in the air, making the night like day. The noise was also terrible.'

After the deafening noise had died down and the acrid fumes of powder blown away, the people feasted their eyes on the illuminations. Myriads of *chiraghs* (oil lamps or *diyas*), lanterns and other kinds of illuminations decorated the walls, palaces and pavilions from the ground all the way up to the top. 'Methought it made a brave and pleasant show,' Mundy added, as the lights died down and the city people found their way home through the dark winding streets, tired, elated and satisfied. Unquestionably, the Mughal empire was the greatest show on earth.

In the fort, feasting continued well into the night. Asaf Khan, the emperor's father-in-law, did not have far to go. His palace was nearest to the fort. The bearers of his gilt palanquin moved with rhythmic steps down the ramps, as the gates were thrown open to allow the cavalcade to pass. His guards took the lead, their tall spears glinting in the light of burning torches held aloft in the deep night. Other grandees followed – the governor, Mahabat Khan, and then perhaps the distinguished Kachwaha, Raja Man Singh. Ordinarily he would have passed Asaf Khan's palace, Todar Mal's mahal and other garden houses along the river. But he had given his own garden to his relative, the emperor. A great tomb was being built there, still covered with scaffolding – the future Taj Mahal. It is time now to leave ephemeral pomp, which turns to dust, and salute the more enduring grandeur of Agra's monuments and the ineffable beauty of the Taj.

---

1   Sambhar lake was then, and still is, an important source of salt.

2   Mir Barr-u-Bahr was the minister responsible for Works and Admiralty, or rather river barges and also the emperor's pilgrim ships bound for Mecca.

3   A pahar is three hours, a measure of time still widely prevalent in north India.

4 Butea monosperma, or Flame of the Forest. D.V. Cohen says: 'The palas is sacred to the moon and to Brahma and said to have sprung from the feather of a falcon impregnated with the Soma, the beverage of the Gods, and thus immortalised' (*Flowering Trees and Shrubs in India*, 1969).

5 A crystal curved like a convex lens, acting as a magnifying glass.

6 One tola is equivalent to 11.6 grams.

the master builders

After Babur committed his dynasty to permanent dominion in Hindustan, developments of the utmost significance followed in art, architecture and, indeed, in cultural life generally. As with earlier conquerors, the Islamic culture of Persia and Central Asia, which the Mughals brought with them, was absorbed in the Indian experience. Hardly thirty years after their initial conquest, Akbar deliberately accelerated the process of cultural synthesis. The momentum it was given never flagged, despite the freeze to which it was subjected in Aurangzeb's reign.

The great works of architecture the Mughals created are the most striking and tangible expression of the cultural synthesis. Scattered all over their empire, but mostly in the capitals and principal cities, the largest and unquestionably the finest concentration is to be found in Agra and Fatehpur Sikri. Although the ground plans of mosques, tombs and gardens were almost invariably conventional, the superstructures gave ample scope to the Indian genius for arrangement of masses and surface and interior decoration.

To a large extent, the unique achievements of the new synthesis were possible because of the wealth of skilled talent and the materials freely available in Hindustan in contrast to the Islamic world of West Asia. Dazzling white marble, sandstone in a variety of lustrous tones, and an abundant cornucopia of precious and semi-precious stones lent themselves to a brilliant new range of architectural expression. In purpose, plan and essential components, the mosques and tombs remained Islamic. In execution, the architecture inspired by the Mughal dynasty is as Indian as the paintings of their ateliers. In music and dance, the Hindustani contribution eclipsed the more robust musicology brought by the Mughals from Central Asia. In poetry, Persian models set the style. After they had mastered the Persian language, Hindustani literati proved themselves nearly as adept, especially in the prose medium. As a return compliment, many of the Mughal conquerors, such as Abdur Rahim *Khan-i-Khanan* and Dara Shikoh, became accomplished Sanskrit scholars and poets in Hindi. One of the clearest expressions of the growth of a syncretic Indian culture was the development of the intermediate language of the camp, Urdu. It gave birth to a rich literature of its own in the succeeding centuries.

The Fort

Agra fort is the epitome of development in architecture, which for sheer range and excellence has few equals anywhere in the world. The fort itself established the model for Mughal forts built after it. Within its walls may be seen a veritable museum of architectural styles, starting with Akbar's Jahangiri Mahal, in red sandstone and wholly indigenous in style, and ending with outstanding examples of the high noon of the Mughal master-builder, his grandson Shah Jahan.

Like his great ancestors Timur and Ulugh Beg, Akbar was a compulsive builder. In 1565, he decided that 'an impregnable fort should be built of hewn stones' that would be 'worthy of the dignity of his dominions.' The foundations, Abul Fazl tells us, were laid 'in an hour, which was supreme for establishing a fortress.' According to tradition, the participation in the ceremony of the Rajput raja of neighbouring Kiraoli was necessary to ensure that the fort would be protected from erosion by the river. We may be sure that Akbar, as always, was punctilious in honouring local sentiment. The river has never endangered the sheer walls.

The construction of the Agra fort was Akbar's first great architectural venture in Hindustan. He went about in characteristic style. Three or four thousand 'strong-armed labourers,' Abul Fazl tells us, were employed under the 'faithful superintendence' of Qasim Khan. Work must have proceeded at a furious pace, with the emperor himself, in his usual way, keeping architects and builders on their toes. The great Hathi Pol gate facing the city bears the inscription; 'Binai-dar-i bihisht,' a chronogram for AH 974, meaning that the

Gates of Paradise were built in the year AD 1565. Four years later the Rajput empress from Amber was able to occupy Bengali Mahal adjoining the Naqqar Khana, or Drum House, overlooking the south gate. Most of the buildings were complete in eight years.

The stone slabs in the walls, Abul Fazl claims, 'were so joined together that the end of a hair could not find a place between them.' This is not just the kind of picturesque exaggeration with which Abul Fazl decorated his chronicle. The Jesuit, Monserrate, who spent two years at Akbar's court from 1580, was almost as enthusiastic. 'The stones of these buildings are so cunningly fitted that the joints are scarcely visible, although no lime was used to fix them together. The beautiful colour of the stone, which is all red, also produces the same effect of uniform solidity.' According to Abul Fazl, more than five hundred red sandstone buildings were erected in the fort, 'in the fine styles of Bengal and Gujarat.' When the whole complex was complete, it may not have been the most beautiful, but it certainly was the most imposing monument in Agra.

Almost invariably the chronicles give different estimates of cost. Abul Fazl puts it at 35 lakh of rupees while Badauni says it was 'about three crores,' or nearly ten times as much. He tells us, too, that to meet the cost Akbar 'ordered a tax of the value of three *sers* of corn on every *jarib* (a square of 60 Akbari yards) of land in the district and appointed collectors and officers from the amirs who held *jagirs* to collect it.'

As may be expected, Akbar's fort outshone the many other buildings that sprang up around it. Abul Fazl says it was 'the best building in the city. The foundation of delightful buildings were laid. The house of Bairam Khan was given to Munim Khan *Khan-i-Khanan*. All the other courtiers and servants commenced to build pleasant houses on both banks of the Yamuna and so the city became adorned.'

Thirty years earlier, Babur and his *begs* had hurriedly built themselves gardens and houses, mostly on the left bank of the river, facing the old city. The building of Akbar's capital, on both banks, was the real beginning of the Mughal city of Agra. The fort itself, as Monserrate shrewdly observes, was both palace and citadel, 'as big as a great city.' The massive walls were never seriously tested. They could have been carried by a breach followed by an impetuous charge, as Akbar himself took the great Rajput fortress of Chitor. Agra fell easily to Sayyid Husain Ali Khan in 1719 and the Marathas in 1785. Its defenders tamely capitulated to Lord Lake's forces in 1803, while the Hindu fort of Bharatpur, not forty miles away, resisted repeated British attacks and did not yield till many years later.

The fort had yet another purpose. 'After it was completed,' says Badauni in his *Muntakhab*, 'it became the depository and store-house of all the gold of Hindustan.' This function was expressed in the Persian chronogram: 'The fortress was built for the sake of gold.' The chronicler also had no compunctions about revealing the location of the hoard. 'The court of the said hall (Daulatkhana-i-khas, to the south of the Diwan-i-khas) ... has under it chambers wherein is the treasure of *ashrafis* (gold mohurs).' Citadel, palace and treasure-house – these were the fort's three main functions.

As Akbar conceived it, the fort was the hub of his empire, complete with all the trappings of majesty. This imperial splendour was greatly magnified by Akbar's grandson, Shah Jahan. Most of the red sandstone buildings that Akbar had constructed in the fort were demolished to make way for the decorated marble palaces characteristic of Shah Jahan's taste in architecture.

Mulla Abdul Hamid Lahori's *Badshah Nama*, the authoritative contemporary account of Shah Jahan's reign, puts it like this: 'By the command of His Majesty (Akbar), were built in that heaven-like fort, lofty buildings of red sandstone for royal residence. As in this everlasting reign (Shah Jahan's) the demand for arts has a different market and the Divine care has adopted a new method of embellishing the world, at the place of the old have been built sky-touching mansions of marble.'

During the ensuing war of succession between Shah Jahan's sons, the eldest, Dara Shikoh, reputedly carried away six crores of treasure to support his gamble for the throne. When he had triumphed over his three brothers, Aurangzeb invaded the fort and parleyed with his father for his collection of priceless jewels. Aurangzeb bided his time in Delhi, until his imprisoned father died in his own marble palaces in 1666. His favourite elephant, Khaliq Dad, died the same day. Shah Jahan's eldest daughter, Jahanara, who had remained at his side till the end, was eventually reconciled with her brother, the Emperor Aurangzeb, and delivered the jewels to him. When Sayyid Husain Ali Khan put an end to Neckusiyar's vain bid for the throne in 1719, he dipped deeply into what remained of the imperial treasure. He also carried away the fabulous sheet of pearls made at Shah Jahan's behest, that was to be placed over his wife's grave in the Taj every Friday.

The fort has suffered more than any other Mughal monument from conquest, plunder and misguided restoration. During their occupation in 1764, the Jats pillaged much of the pietra dura inlay. They carried away marble tanks and reservoirs from Machhi Bhawan to their palace in Deeg. A ball fired in General Perron's cannonade in 1803 tore through the screen of a small courtyard in front of the Diwan-i-khas. Baths of great beauty were wrenched out by the British and sent as a present to that old roué, the Prince Regent, later William IV. Worst of all, a considerable number of decorative marble pieces were sold by auction in the 1830s in the time of the Governor-General, Lord William Bentinck. Indian merchants united solidly, the marbles fetched only a tenth of the price expected, or the Taj itself was destined for a similar fate. Because of the disappointing outcome, a seriously considered proposal to sell the Taj as scrap was dropped. That most business-like organisation, the honourable East India Company, was impervious to any consideration other than profit.

During the Mutiny of 1857, the British took refuge in the fort. The Lieutenant Governor Colvin, died before relieving forces arrived, and was buried in the courtyard of the Diwan-i-am. His tasteless memorial is completely out of place in this splendid setting. The British then converted the old palace citadel into a strongly garrisoned fortress, complete with outrageously ugly barracks and other buildings in the worst

PWD style. Most of the area inside was given over to these utilitarian purposes, sparing only the south-eastern corner open to visitors today. The gateway to the Jami Masjid was destroyed and Asaf Khan's palace, the finest outside the fort, levelled, along with other mahals and garden pavilions lining the strand all the way to the Taj. Agra was never the same again.

* * *

The lay-out of the fort is relatively simple. The main axis, about 822.96 metres in length, runs parallel to the river Yamuna flowing close by. The walls bulge out westwards in an irregular semi-circle. William Finch, who was in Agra during the reign of Emperor Jahangir, has left an apt description of the sprawling city, which 'lyeth in manner of a half-moon, bellying to the landward.' This exactly describes the form of the fort — rather like a portly gentleman contentedly facing the city.

Of the fort itself, Finch says, 'Upon the banks of the river stands the castle, one of the fairest and admirablest buildings of the East ... enclosed with a fair and strong wall of squared stone; about this is cast a fair ditch, over it drawbridges.' Finch was rather far out as a judge of distance. The fort, he says, was 4.8 or 6.8 kilometres in compass, though the actual perimeter is just 2.4 kilometres.

Although contemporary authors, such as Abul Fazl, Badauni and Khwaja Nizam-ud-din, have given conflicting dimensions of the walls, all three are equally ecstatic about their appearance and majesty. They are about 21.34 metres in height at the highest points while the width at the base cannot be accurately determined because they are embedded in masonry and filling. Battlements, embrasures and other defensive features in vogue at the time are provided. Of the four gates originally built, only two are now open, Hathi Pol, to the north-west and Amar Singh, originally Akbari Gate, to the south. Naqqar Khanas were placed high up in the battlements above these two gates. These proclaimed the arrivals and departures of the emperor, and also his presence in the audience balcony, by the measured beating of several pairs of drums, the clashing of cymbals and the long, bass notes of the *karna*. At first the French physician Bernier found the music rather tedious, but admits, almost regretfully, that he ultimately yielded. 'There are ten or twelve hautboys (from which is derived today's *sehnai*), and as many cymbals, which play together ... the roaring sound ... on my first arrival stunned me so as to be insupportable; but such is the power of habit that this same noise is now heard by me with pleasure; in the night, particularly, when in bed and afar, on my terrace this music sounds in my ears as solemn, grand, and melodious.'

One of the fort's most striking features is its apparent planlessness. Apart from the rivers to the east, there are no distinguishable natural features that a builder could have strengthened by defensive walls. As Akbar's intention was to glorify 'the dignity of his dominions,' his architects might have been expected to have presented him with a more formal ground plan, somewhat on the lines of the imperial camp described by Abul Fazl in the sixteenth Ain. The probable reason why the existing configuration was adopted by Qasim Khan is that he superimposed the new fort on the old.

Jahangir claims that Akbar 'threw down' the old fort and 'founded a fort of cut red stone,' without strictly identifying the site of the new fort in relation to the old. Almost inadvertently, however, Abul Fazl reveals the true position when he says, ... 'an inevitable mandate was issued that the old fort ... should be removed, and in that place should be founded an impregnable palace.' An immense structure, with four centuries of continuous history, could not have disappeared into the ground. The circumstances indicate that Qasim Khan took advantage of the great height of the old fort to give the new fort its distinctive feature of a series of rising planes. He built around and on it, and probably used as much of the material available as he could to ram the foundations and fill the walls; they were then faced with red sandstone and provided with imposing gates.

In his report of 1871, General Cunningham, who was Director-General of the Archaeological Survey of India, has given convincing reasons in support of this view. Earlier, in 1859, he was chief engineer of the North Western Province at Agra. In both capacities he had unrivalled opportunities to submit the matter to technical examination. When embrasures were made for guns in the walls of Amar Singh gate, it took the workmen only four to five days to pierce the outer (Akbari) walls, and no less than a fortnight to complete the same work in the wall of the inner gate. His conclusion was that they were made at different times, adopting different techniques. 'I believe,' he says, 'that the old Pathan fort occupied exactly the same position as that of Akbar, with the exception perhaps of some of the gateway outworks.'

Abul Fazl tells us with a flourish that the walls were 'provided with four gates whereby, the doors of the dominion were opened to the four quarters of the world.' Finch, who spent nearly two years in Agra with Hawkins trying unsuccessfully to outwit the Portuguese at Jahangir's court, is a little more down to earth. Through the north gate, 'you pass to rampire with great pieces, another west to Bazar, called Cichery gate, within which ... is the Casi, his seat of chief justice in matters of law, and by it two or three murtherers very great (one three feet in the bore and fifteen long) of cast brass.' Flanked by statues of elephants, this gate is called Hathi Pol. When Finch saw it, statues of Jaimal and Patta, the two heroic defenders of Chitor, had been placed there by their conqueror, Akbar. A passage within the fort led from Hathi Pol to the south, or Amar Singh Gate, the only one now open, 'with houses and munition all along on both sides.' Here, evidently, was the fort's store of ordnance. 'The fourth gate is to the river, the Dersane (Darshani) leading into a faire court extending alongst the river, in which the king looks forth every morning at sun-rising which hee salutes, and then his nobles resort to their *tessillam*.'

In this passage Finch gives us a glimpse of life in the fort · during Jahangir's reign. Near the *kacheri* (court), where the *kazi* administered the law, was the office of the vizier who 'sits every morning some three hours, by whose hands pass all matters of rents, grants, lands, firmans, debts, etc.' For the public, these two offices were of vital importance. Without the *kazi* there was no redress, and without the vizier there could be no decisions in innumerable matters relating to grants and rights of all kinds of lands. The fourth gate, facing the river, was the place of public *darshan*, where the people were enabled to see the emperor, and offer their deep salaams.

Right under the 'faire court' where Jahangir looked out every morning, 'is a kind of scaffold whereon his nobles stand, but the addees (*ahadis*) with others away below in the court. Here also every noone he looketh forth to behold tamashan (*tamasha*, or show) of fighting elephants, lyons, buffles, killing of deare with leopards, which is a custome on every day of the weeke, Sunday excepted, on which is no fighting, but Tuesday on the contrary is a day of blood, both of fighting beasts and justiced men, the king judging and seeing execution.'

* * *

Today's visitors, unless they are excessively susceptible, are unlikely to be troubled by the shades of 'justiced men.' Entering by Amar Singh Gate, only a fraction of the great space enclosed by Akbar's walls can now be seen; the rest has been closed, originally by the British, to make way for barracks and other military purposes. Of the buildings Akbar made, hardly any exist, except Jahangiri Mahal, the Naqqar Khanas, the ruined traces of Bengali Mahal and his own Akbari Mahal.

A ramp of noble proportions leads up to the level of the court outside Jahangiri Mahal. From the top of the ramp, a path leads back towards the Naqqar Khana and the remains of the two earliest mahals built by Akbar but attention is immediately captured by an exquisite red sandstone palace across the lawns on the right. This is Jahangiri Mahal.

Cunningham is unquestionably right in holding that Jahangiri Mahal was inspired by the Man Mandir Palace in Gwalior. There is a striking identity of design, decoration and principles of construction. Akbar, it is well-known, was deeply influenced by Hindu culture. He had married a Rajput princess as early as 1562 and sent for the celebrated singer Tan Sen from the Gwalior court even before he started construction of his fort. Abul Fazl tells us that he caused buildings to be made in a number of Indian styles. It is surely not straining credibility to suggest that he sent for builders from Gwalior not long after he summoned Tan Sen. Jahangiri Mahal adjoins the area where Akbar built the Bengali and Akbari Mahals, which suggests that it was one of the same group.

The principal features of this exquisite red sandstone palace are the tiled decorations on the front wall, the square domed hall just inside the entrance, and the grand central court which, as Carleylle says, is 'entirely Hindu in character.' Beyond is an open hall with fourteen pillars, supporting bracket capitals, richly carved and ornamented with pendants. 'But the stone roof or ceiling of these pillared halls', says Carleylle, 'is the most remarkable feature about it. It has a narrow, flat, oblong, central compartment resting on four sloping side compartments, and this roof is supported most curiously by stone cross beams, which are ornamented with the quaint device of a great serpent or dragon carved on them lengthways. It is altogether a wonderfully constructed roof, a wonder of architectural constructive ingenuity, unique and without a parallel in its design.' The parallel, however, as Cunningham points out, is with the roofs of the Man Mandir

Palace in Gwalior, built by the Rajput rulers towards the end of the fifteenth century.

The central court is decorated with a panel of bas-reliefs of birds, ducks, parrots and fruits equalled only, in Carleylle's opinion, by some of the ancient Buddhist decorative panels. Carved stone lattices screened off passages from where the ladies of the palace were able to look down. An archway leads into an open porch facing the river, where the doorways are faced with white marble, tastefully carved, and provided with latticed recesses from which it was possible to look out towards the river without being seen from below. As in other Akbari buildings, the marble decorations could have been added by Jahangir, thus associating his name with this distinctively Akbari palace.

Cleanly cut and fantastically carved, the lustrous red sandstone of Jahangiri Mahal strikingly contrasts with the domed and marbled pavilions built by Shah Jahan further to the north. Originally, the whole area within the walls was covered by the five hundred buildings in Gujarati, Bengali and other indigenous styles constructed in obedience to Akbar's command. Jahangir also built a palace for himself. This, he tells us in his *Tuzuk*, 'rests upon the gate (Darshani), which opens on the river Yamuna and is supported by twenty-five pillars, all covered with plates of gold, and all inlaid with rubies, turquoises and pearls.' It was in this pleasurable place that Jahangir entertained his friends at wine parties, and from which he viewed animal fights in the strand below. Shah Jahan had other ideas. In his craze for marble, Shah Jahan cleared the whole area, as far as Moti Masjid, of the buildings erected with such care and refinement of taste by his two predecessors. Only Jahangiri Mahal was spared. This was done, Mulla Abdul Hamid tells us, because, 'the said buildings were not liked by the critical disposition of the world-maintaining and art-spreading Emperor (Shah Jahan ...) They were demolished in this august reign' to make way for his marble creations.

The first of these was 'a new marble building, extremely delightful ... consisting of an octagonal chamber ... the five sides of which overlook the river, and are adorned, well-painted and delightful.' This is none other than the beautiful Samman Burj, or Octagonal Tower, commonly, and surely more appropriately called the Jasmin Tower. It replaced the Shah Burj in which Jahangir had hung his golden bells of justice. The Diwan-i-am, Daulatkhana-i-khas, Khas Mahal and other palaces and pavilions were completed by the time Shah Jahan returned from the Deccan in 1635. The dado reliefs and pietra dura inlay done in these buildings during the intervening years belong to the same period as the exquisite work in the Taj Mahal. Pillaged during the Jat occupation, they are now exposed to constant streams of visitors, yet the elegant Jasmin Tower still represents the quintessence of Shah Jahan's age of magnificence.

One of the earliest buildings to be completed was the Diwan-i-am. The walled courtyard and cloisters are all that remain of Akbar's original. According to Muhammad Saleh, canopies were stretched over the courtyard, but Shah Jahan ordered construction of a *chihl satun* (hall supported by forty pillars) in front of the *jharoka*. Muhammad Saleh adds that the hall, the Diwan-i-am seen there today, was 'so well built of red sandstone, covered with shell-plaster by the labour of wonder-working mathematicians, that it excites the emulation of the dawn of morning.' Hyperbole notwithstanding, the colonnaded Diwan-i-am is superbly proportioned and finished, despite the whitewash of early British rulers and subsequent inept restoration. According to the same author, it was enclosed by two rails — an inner one of silver, as high as a man, and an outer, stone *katahra* (fence), with openings for entrance. These elegant features replaced the simpler red inner rail and the plain outer rail that had served in the two previous reigns. The Akbari sandstone *jharoka*, says Mulla Abdul Hamid, was rebuilt by Shah Jahan in marble, inlaid with precious stones of various colours, 'and the ceiling embossed with gold and made a counterpart of the roof of heaven.'

Further east, and completely separated from the Hall of Public Audience by the large courtyard of Machhi Bhawan, is the beautifully proportioned double-pillared hall of the Diwan-i-khas. A Persian inscription in Nastaliq characters in the south wall opens with the lines.

The erection of this delightful lofty palace
Has exalted Akbarabad to the Arsh (ninth Heaven),

a claim which the admiring visitor might be inclined to concede. The open terrace opposite the Diwan-i-khas was originally covered, but the hall was dismantled by the Jats and the materials carried away to decorate their own palaces. On the open balcony is one of the last surviving relics of Jahangir's reign, the throne hewn out of a single block of black marble. Its sides are inscribed with adulatory lines in Persian. The credulous maintain that when it was mounted by the Jat ruler, it cracked from side to side and blood gushed out! The red discolouration is due to nothing more alarming than the presence of iron in the marble.

Between the Diwan-i-am and Diwan-i-khas is the Machhi Bhawan, or what Mulla Abdul Hamid called 'the Lower-Court.' The Jats left hardly anything of its imperial splendour. 'On three sides,' says the Mulla, 'have been built lofty stone edifices and offices, wherein is chiefly the treasure of precious gems and fine instruments set with precious stones.' Miraculously, one thing at least escaped their marauding hands. Along the southern wall is 'an umbrella embossed pavilion of white marble on four pillars in extreme elaboration and purity. In this pavilion the golden throne, exalted like the seventh Heaven, is honoured by His Majesty's seat on it.' It is as perfect as the dome of Brunelleschi's Pazzi Chappel. No more fitting place for the celebrated Peacock Throne can be imagined.

Behind the Diwan-i-khas Shah Jahan built himself the most luxurious building in the fort, his Daulatkhana-i-khas. It includes a Tambi Khana (Parlour), with marble walls decorated by 'various paintings and adorned with gold.' The parlour, with its sunk marble pool, is unsurpassed for the refinement of its decoration. Close by is the Jasmin Tower. Shah Jahan is said to have gazed at the reflection of the Taj in a mirror inlaid in one of its pillars.

Further south is the Khas Mahal, where Jahanara Begum lived in a style that the grandest of the empresses would have envied. Facing the Khas Mahal is a large court called Angoori Bagh, best described by Mulla Abdul Hamid. 'Before it is a waterfall and in front a garden like Paradise, whose four plots are full of various kinds of flowers and odoriferous herbs.' The Angoori Bagh of today hardly comes up to the chronicler's description.

The *Hammam* was one of the acknowledged gems of the fort. According to Mulla Abdul Hamid, it consisted of several buildings overlooking the river. They were fitted with all the luxuries expected of the most magnificent of the Mughals. There were fountains, cold and hot baths and 'Aleppo glasses that have been so disposed that the river and river side gardens are in view.' What is left of the baths, after the best marbles were sent to the Prince Regent, is now closed to the public.

Also closed until recently was the Palace of Mirrors, or Shish Mahal. Light flashes back from the tiny pieces of glass set in patterns in the roof and walls. The effect of this fairy display is heightened when a water jet spills into the marble basins, which have been designed to create the illusion of swimming fish. Mimic waterfalls, lighted from within, produce effects in the mirrors that are totally enchanting.

It is difficult to conceive anything more beautiful, but a monument that is heavenly in its purity of line awaits the visitor to the north-west of the Diwan-i-khas. In an elevated courtyard, hidden away from the rest of the fort, is the finest gem of all, the Moti Masjid. The name, Pearl Mosque, is an accepted convention for a white marble place of prayer intended for the emperor, his family and close attendants. There are Pearl

Mosques in the forts at Delhi and Lahore. From afar only the three domes and corner *chhattris* are visible. Coming upon it at the end of a line of steps and a simple gateway, the effect of this poem in white marble is, as the Urdu phrase has it, beyond words. A triple row of pillars, strung together with delicate Persian arches, supports the roof of a single hall, 45.72 metres long and 18.29 metres broad.

An elegant fountain in the middle of the courtyard is intended for ablutions before prayers. Side rooms, screened by marble lattices, are provided for ladies of the harem. One of the lines from the inscription in the entablature over the front row of pillars compares the great red sandstone fort of Akbarabad with 'a halo round the shining moon.' It was completed in 1653 and had taken seven years to be made, at a cost of three lakh rupees. 'As the capital of Akbarabad,' says Muhammad Saleh, 'had not for a long time gained the fortune ... of the favour-bestowing visit,' Shah Jahan travelled from Delhi by boat to see 'the shining moon.' The view of its domes and finials across the courtyard of Machhi Bhawan must have consoled him in his long confinement until his death in 1666.

Aurangzeb set apart the Nagina Masjid, a still smaller mosque, for the ladies of the court. It is approached by a passage from the north-west corner of Machhi Bhawan. Close by is a beautiful balcony with a courtyard lined with apartments in red sandstone. This is the Mina Bazaar, where court ladies traded trinkets with the emperor and his courtiers. Here Nur Jahan is said to have charmed the impressionable Prince Salim, a passion that profoundly influenced the fortunes of the dynasty.

Despite the beauty of the Shah Jahani additions, Agra fort preeminently expresses Akbar's majestic sense of empire. Its imposing red sandstone walls contain exquisite marble mosques and palaces, gracious courtyards, elegant pavilions and the finest reliefs and inlays, yet it always remains the great red fort of Akbarabad. For sheer presence it has no rival in India.

Details from Akbar's tomb at Sikandra.

An aerial view of the entrance of Akbar's tomb at Sikandra, ten km from Agra.

Agra and its environs bear the stamp of Akbar, where he built not only a massive fort but also a palace and city complex. The gateway to his mausoleum at Sikandra.

The white marble courtyard containing the delicately carved sepulchre of Akbar at Sikandra, near Agra, sits on top of three storeys of red sandstone pavilions. A view from one corner of the entrance courtyard.

Details from the facade of Itmad-ud-Daulah's tomb. The Moghul art of inlay work that covers all its walls was perfected here. Different colours of precious stone inlay have been used to create geometrical designs and floral motifs, with outstanding effect.

The tomb of Itmad-ud-Daulah was designed by his daughter, the empress Nur Jahan, and completed in 1628. It is a platform tomb with four short minarets and epitomizes a perfect synthesis of Indian and Islamic architectural elements.

The lower burial chamber with the two gravestones of Mirza Ghiyas Beg (father of Nur Jahan and prime minister of Jahangir) and his wife, Asmat Begum, in Itmad-ud-Daulah's mausoleum in Agra. Asmat Begum's tomb lies at the centre of the chamber, while the nobleman was buried by her side-a pattern that was replicated in the Taj Mahal. The subdued light entering through the latticed screen imparts an appropriate sobriety to the chamber. There is an exceptional display of marble inlay work on the walls in striking geometric and flowing designs.

Shah Jahan died in the winter of 1665. His body was brought down from the fort through the watergate to the river Jamuna. The cortege sailed solemnly to the Taj Mahal where he was buried next to his beloved wife. On the opposite bank of the river from the Taj are the ruins of an old foundation where Shah Jahan had intended to build a mausoleum for himself replicating the Taj. But Aurangzeb ordered that his father be buried next to his mother, thwarting Shah Jahan's plans.

FATEHPUR SIKRI

An aerial view of Fatehpur Sikri, Akbar's capital city for fifteen years, built as his grateful offering to the Sufi saint, Sheikh Salim Chisti, who had prophesied the birth of heirs to the emperor. In the spacious courtyard of Fatehpur's Jama Masjid stands the holy marble shrine of the saint.

Next page: The central sandstone pillar of the Diwan-i-Khas or Hall of Private Audience at Fatehpur Sikri. Featuring intricately carved brackets, it supports the platform seat of the emperor in the centre, as well as the four bridges that radiate from it to the balconies on the sides. A marvel as a work of craftsmanship, its purpose, it is believed, was to provide seclusion for discussions between the emperor and his "nine jewels" (navratans) - Tansen, Birbal, Todar Mal, Abul Fazl, Bhagwantdas, Abdul Rahim Mansingh, among others - seated in the balconies.

fatehpur sikri:
a place of victory

While Akbar was returning from his yearly pilgrimage to Ajmer in the rainy season of 1571, he halted at Sikri. 'Now that his standards had arrived at the place,' says Abul Fazl, 'his former design was pressed forward and an order was issued that the superintendents of affairs should erect lofty buildings for the special use of the *shahinshah* ... His Majesty gave it the name of Fatehbad (place of victory) and this by common use was made into Fatehpur.' The victory that inspired this name was Akbar's celebrated conquest of Gujarat.

If the visitor should turn northwards before passing through Agra gate of Akbar's new capital, he will discover the old town of Sikri, nestling at the foot of the hill. Though a modest place, Sikri was not merely pre-Mughal, but pre-Muslim. The Sikarwar Rajputs who had settled there built temples, and must have created the original lake by damming the watercourse. Medieval Rajputs were renowned for these skills. The first wave of Muslim conquerors, at the end of the twelfth and early thirteenth centuries, used the stones of the temples to build their mosques, as they had done before at the Qutb Minar complex in Delhi. When Akbar decided to establish his capital at Fatehpur, he built the Terah Mori (Thirteen Gates) dam that remained intact until damaged by floods a few years ago.

Babur had been enchanted by the lake. While reconnoitering the terrain before the battle against Rana Sanga, says Babur, 'it crossed my mind that the well-watered ground for a large camp was at Sikri.' Accordingly, a party was despatched 'to look for a camping ground on the bank of the Sikri lake.'

After his victory at Kanwaha, Babur spent two days supervising construction of a garden in Sikri, and had a pavilion built for his pleasure in the lake itself. With characteristic candour, he adds: 'We went over by boat, had an awning set up on it and elected for *majun,*' his favourite drugged confection. A well made for the garden bears the inscription: 'At the command of Zahir-ud-din Muhammad Babur, Badshah Ghazi, may God perpetuate his realm and rule. The construction of this well was, through the Divine grace, completed in the year 1527 (AH 933), after (he) had returned conquering and victorious from his campaign against the misbelieving Rana Sanga.' The Rajput descendants of Sikri's medieval inhabitants will tell the visitor that the field of Kanwaha is still red because of the uparalleled carnage of that hard fought Mughal victory.

The Sufi saint, Sheikh Salim Chishti, chose a place for his cell at the western summit of the ridge, far from the distractions of the little town. Akbar seems to have conceived the idea of doing honour to him, ever since the saint's intercession had blessed him with the birth of his three eldest sons, Salim and Murad in Sikri and Daniyal in Ajmer. 'My revered father,' Jahangir noted in his memoirs, 'considering the village of Sikri, which was the place of my birth, lucky for him, made it his capital.' At last he had the opportunity. The empire rested on firm foundations, and court ceremonies reflected the glory of the most powerful of the Mughal emperors. Akbar was in his fortieth year. His keen zest for life never slackened, though his earlier exertions ensured him a peaceful span of fourteen years at the capital on the hill.

In July 1585, his half-brother, Mirza Muhammad Hakim, died in Kabul. Further north, a possible Uzbeg threat was developing. Akbar furled his standards and promptly set out for Lahore. During the fourteen years he was there, Akbar struck out to confirm his hold on Kabul, and to bring Qandahar, Sind and Kashmir within the empire. Akbar's interest then turned southwards; affairs in the Deccan demanded his attention. In 1598, Akbar once again established himself in Darul-Khilafat, as Abul Fazl had described Agra.

Akbar's stay in Fatehpur marked a distinct phase in his life. It was while he was here that the distinctive features of

89

Mughal administration, based on arrangements for collection of land revenue, were perfected by Raja Todar Mal and other distinguished imperial servants and enforced throughout the empire. In 1579, the dramatic claim was made of the emperor's ultimate authority in religious affairs, once again from the halls of Fatehpur. Though the spiritual order was eclipsed even in his lifetime, some of Akbar's temporal institutions still survive, just as surely as the foundations of his 'sublime fortress' of Agra have defied the corrosive hand of time. The cords that held the empire together reached down from the Daulat Khana palace on the Aravalli outcrop to the farthest *parganas* of the empire.

In 1591, while Akbar was in Lahore, he sent Abul Fazl's elder brother, the poet Faizi, on a mission to the Deccan. Faizi spent a few days at Fatehpur and informed the emperor that though the royal buildings were being properly cared for by Ibrahim, nephew of Sheikh Salim Chishti, the houses of the nobles were decaying through neglect. Even five years had made a difference. Akbar himself had no further use for Fatehpur. He paid only a brief visit in 1601, on his return from the Deccan, and the neglected town was left to itself by his successors.

Jahangir was an involuntary occupant of the deserted capital in 1619. When he returned from the south, plague was raging in Agra. Prudence demanded that until the epidemic abated the court should give it a wide berth. For the three months Jahangir was there, Sikri recalled some of its lost splendour. Prince Khurram's solar birthday weighing ceremony was observed, and *Nauroz* was celebrated with undiminished magnificence. In Agra, 38.4 kilometres away, Jahangir tells us in his memoirs, 'daily about 100 people, more or less, were dying' of the plague. For a brief spell the refined elegance of Akbar's court had given way to wanton display and ill-timed extravagance.

Therefore, Fatehpur was left to its fate. Fortunately, the Sheikh's descendants and the *mujahirs* (caretakers) looked after the sacred place and palaces as well as they could; but the *mahals* of the nobles have disappeared, the stones being used by the people to construct their own houses. The only exceptions are Todar Mal's *baradari* and Hada Rani's *mahal*, both far out near the city wall. The Jats carried away whatever took their fancy, and after the British set up an administrative centre at Fatehpur in the middle of the nineteenth century, more stone and rubble were pounded into the earth to make roads. The new rulers, in a tidying up operation of amazing insensitivity, made a road through the Diwan-i-am and removed screens, tore down some walls and blocked a number of passages. The seraglio was the principal victim of these unwanted attentions. At the end of the nineteenth century, the Viceroy, Lord Curzon, retrieved the whole complex from oblivion, and instituted measures that preserved whatever we see there today.

* * *

When Akbar decided to build himself a capital in Sikri, the great tented camp, described by Abul Fazl in the sixteenth *Ain*, must have been pitched nearby. Very likely he chose 'the well-watered ground' where Babur had camped before giving battle to Rana Sanga at Kanwaha. Akbar himself

91

had devised the trappings of the camp. Its centrepiece, the Gulal-bar, was a 'grand enclosure, the invention of His Majesty, the doors of which are made very strong, and secured with locks and keys. It is never less than one hundred yards square.' Around it were a series of pavilions, tents and enclosures, many of them richly decorated. A two-storeyed pavilion was erected, 'in which His Majesty performs divine worship, and from the top of which he receives the compliments of the nobility. No one connected with the seraglio enters this building without special leave.' Nearby were twenty-four apartments, 'where the favourite women reside,' and a place for the *Urdu begis* and other servants. A Diwan-i-am, Diwan-i-khas and Naqqar Khana for the imperial band, and even privies, called by the Chaghatai name of *ibachki*, made up the rest of its principal features. Finally, towering above, the *akash diya* illuminated the emperor's quarters at night.

The imperial camp was frozen in stone in the new capital. Akbar made skilful use of the jagged features of the Aravalli hills. The elaborate web of forms yielded to the asymmetries of the natural setting. They were laid out in palace, pavilion and cloister as if nature herself had fashioned them to match the rugged hills of Braj.[1] Red sandstone and mortar, annealed by age, in forms that are neither distinctively Islamic in conception nor entirely indigenous in execution, but an outstandingly successful blend of both, enfold the spine of the hill with a sensitivity to the environment rarely achieved in the long history of town planning in the Indian peninsula.

Fatehpur is stamped with the refined simplicity characteristic of its creator. The place of honour on the summit of the hill was reserved for the Jami Masjid and the exquisite tomb Akbar made for Sheikh Salim Chishti. The brilliance of this small gem, subsequently veneered with chaste white marble by Jahangir, is enhanced by being placed in a setting of unadorned sandstone. Though often carved into fantastic forms, and the surfaces chiselled in patterns of breath-taking intricacy, the stone of Akbar's city speaks for itself. There is no trace in Fatehpur of the luxurious aestheticism of his son Jahangir or the often florid opulence of Shah Jahan. Much more than Agra, to which Shah Jahan gave the name Akbarabad, the capital on the hill deserves to be linked with his name.

Though Akbar himself was the animating spirit of the entire town plan, there can be no question that he was assisted by the finest talent in the empire. Nowhere is this more apparent than in the arrangement of the principal buildings, the sensitive response to the character of the environment, and the unmistakably Akbari character of the construction. The materials used were almost exclusively stone and the finest quality of mortar. Monserrate, who arrived early in 1580, long after the main work was complete, maintains that the emperor sometimes worked alongside the builders. With such an example the amirs could hardly afford to be left behind. The fever of construction spread rapidly. As Abul Fazl says, 'all grades of officers and the public generally, made dwellings for themselves, and a high wall of stone and lime was placed round the place.'

Most of the important imperial buildings were apparently ready and in use in the first year or two. Other buildings followed: the great Buland Darwaza was completed in 1576, and the bazaar was ready soon afterwards. 'In a short time,' says Abul Fazl, 'there was a great city, and there were charming palaces. Benevolent institutions, such as *khanquas* (seminaries), schools and baths, were also constructed, and a large stone bazaar was built. Beautiful gardens were made in the vicinity. A place of great concourse was brought together such as might move the envy of the world.' Abul Fazl little knew that he was describing one of the most exciting examples of town planning and construction anywhere in the contemporary world.

In the early years there must have been an inelegant scramble amongst the courtiers for builders and workmen. Inexhaustible supplies of stone, however, could be quarried in nearby Tantpur and Rupbas, and in Sikri itself. Like the dockleaf that grows near nettle, a colony of stone-cutters had established themselves in Sikri. With the main work in Agra fort complete, in the winter of 1571-72, they were free to comply with the emperor's command to build his new capital.

Although Fatehpur was constructed at hurricane speed, quality was never sacrificed. The purity of design and excellence of stone cutting are unmatched. Equally striking is the sense of restraint that kept the execution of the plan within the ambit of the emperor's original conception. Fatehpur was intended as an act of veneration to the saint whose intercession had blessed him with sons. Planes rose and fell away, but soaring high above all, the immense arch of Buland Darwaza, the gateway to the house of God, raised a delicate filigree of cupolas against the sky.

Another distinctive feature of Fatehpur is that it is entirely Akbar's own capital. In Agra fort, little now remains that is specifically Akbari. Except for the change to marble in the tomb of the saint by Jahangir, his successors left it untouched. The Akbari imprint is clearly apparent in the blending of Islamic and indigenous traditions, the skilful setting of the various civic elements that constituted one of the most populous medieval capitals in the world, and the dominance of what today would be called the master plan.

When Akbar set up his camp in Sikri towards the end of 1571, the kilometre long ridge itself was bare. Sheikh Salim Chishti's hermitage was at the western end, and when the saint returned from his last pilgrimage to Mecca in 1564, the stone-cutters of Sikri built him a mosque. Called the Stone-cutter's Mosque, it was the first building on the hill. When the Rajput empress from Amber was enceinte, a small palace was built for her next to the Sheikh's *khanquah*. The Rang Mahal (Palace of Delight), as it is called, is now much neglected. From there the escarpment fell away.

With these buildings at the western end of the ridge, and the old town at the foot to the north-east, the problem of setting the capital's new buildings was automatically resolved. The highest point at the western end was reserved for the Jami Masjid and the tomb of the saint. He had died in February 1572, soon after Akbar moved to Sikri. Reverence for his memory persuaded Akbar to complete the project. The imperial palaces, the seraglio and offices were aligned with the Masjid, slightly athwart the axis of the ridge. Sites were given to the highest ranking nobles between the palaces and Agra gate to the east, where the ridge merges with the surrounding plain.

The bazaar, a necessary facility in an imperial city with all manner of needs, ran along the foot of the hill and beyond, to the south-east. The lesser nobility, and late-comers like Raja Todar Mal, had to be content with whatever land was left. The revenue minister was no laggard as a courtier. He had been sent to Gujarat to overhaul the administration after it was conquered. On his return, the best he could get for his *baradari*² was a place at the southern corner, near the city wall. Large intervening areas must have been occupied by the mahals of the nobility, stables for the emperor's animals, quarters for the keepers, guards, palace women and the vast concourse of serving men and workers in the imperial *karkhanahs. Lashkars* (regiments) of cavalry and infantry must have been quartered close by. Except for the sacred buildings and the imperial complex that were cared for by the Sheikh's descendants, hardly any vestige remains of the great medieval city. It is haunted by the glories of the past.

In keeping with Islamic tradition, the imperial buildings, as in the Alhambra at Granada, formed three groups – the palaces, the seraglio and the royal offices – each distinct yet closely interrelated. As the living presence of the emperor was Fatehpur's cynosure, so was the Daulat Khana (Abode of Fortune) the focus of the town plan. The heart of the Daulat Khana, or Imperial Residence, was the Diwankhana-i-khas and the apartment on the floor above, called Khilwatkada-i-khas or

Khwabgah (Dream House, or Sleeping Chamber). No one could enter the emperor's apartments without being summoned. Ladies from the harem had to wait until they were called, and not even the most respected amir would have attempted to enter without the emperor's express invitation.

As dawn broke, Akbar would appear at the *jharoka* in the southern wall of the Diwankhana-i-khas overlooking the courtyard of the Daftarkhana. The *darshaniyas*[3] would have been admitted by the palace guards to make the obeisance. This done, 'His Majesty allows the attendants of the harem to pay their compliments. During this time various matters of worldly and religious import are brought to the notice of His Majesty.'

Akbar then descended from the Khwabgah, where he slept, to the ground floor of the Diwankhana-i-khas. Here he transacted business with his ministers and closest counsellors, taking care to consult those present before announcing his decisions. As he went along the passages past Anup Talao (Peerless Pool), ten pairs of drums in the Naqqar Khana started beating a tattoo. It was now three hours after sunrise. The courtiers in the Diwan-i-am were on their feet, ready to make the *kornish*. By this time the emperor had moved through the small formal garden to the pavilion in the western wall of the Diwan-i-am. There he settled down amongst costly carpets and jewelled cushions. A deep obeisance was performed; the assembly had received the emperor's *darshan*. Now he could listen and impart justice.

Monserrate vividly describes the scene. He and his companions spent two years in Fatehpur in a despairing effort to win the elusive emperor's conversion. 'It is hard,' Monserrate says, 'to exaggerate how accessible he (Akbar) makes himself to all who wish audience of him. For he creates an opportunity almost every day for any of the common people to see him and converse with him, and he endeavours to show himself pleasant-spoken and affable rather than severe toward all who come to speak with him.' The court 'is always thronged with multitudes of men of every type,' for Akbar 'is specially remarkable for his love of keeping great crowds of people around him.' The emperor's popularity was apparently unbounded; but justice had its grimmer side. An executioner stood by with instruments of torture. These were never actually used while the Jesuits were at court. Condemned prisoners were taken away to be despatched elsewhere, whether by execution, impalement or trampling by elephants.

Further west of the Diwan-i-am is the main courtyard in the palace complex. There is now little to suggest the scenes of splendour that visitors to the court witnessed in Fatehpur's brief hey day. The bare stone was strewn with luxurious carpets, woven in the imperial workshops, *kannats* made of hand-block prints from Gujarat were set up as partitions, awnings were stretched across the courtyard, and the stone rings that held them may still be seen along the top-most course. If he held court elsewhere than in the Diwan-i-am, the *awrang*, or 'throne', studded with precious stones, was placed under a *chatr* (umbrella). On days of festivity, as in battle, the *alam* (standard), followed the emperor as he came out, with the *qur* (flags and other insignia) unfurled.

A *pachisi* board, embedded in the stone floor of the

courtyard with a roughly fashioned stone seat in the middle, is strangely out of place in this majestic setting. *Pachisi* is a kind of ludo, played with cowrie shells. Akbar, seated on the stone seat is said to have used slave-girls as pieces in costumes of different colours. This story is as apocryphal as the suggestion that the emperor played blind man's buff in the nearby building of Ankh Michauli. There is not a shred of contemporary evidence to support the inference that Akbar indulged in such juvenile diversions. Badauni would not have hesitated to pour his scorn into the *Muntakhab*, nor would Monserrate, smarting from the discomfiture of his failure as an evangelist, have omitted to make some reference to such evidence of frailty.

It has been suggested that *pachisi* and *ankh michauli* were most likely to have been diversions of the young Muhammad Shah, who was an aspirant to the throne in the uncertain years after Aurangzeb's death. The powerful Sayyid brothers were at their familiar game of king-making, and permitted their ward to amuse himself for a while in Fatehpur before they put him on the throne. Akbar is as likely to have made a *pachisi* court in the principal imperial courtyard as Louis XIV would be to permit boule in the Tuileries, or Queen Victoria a game of racquets in Buckingham Palace.

Ankh Michauli was actually a treasury, or rather part of a treasury, because a larger building to the west of it, which collapsed in 1892, is believed to have been a repository of copper coins. Ankh Michauli is lined with recesses which were covered with sliding slabs of stone. It is thought that gold and silver coins were stored in them, and that the gallery between the inner and outer walls was meant for guards on patrol. The roof of the central room is supported by struts, whose lower ends are shaped as heads of monsters and whose mouths disgorge serpentine scrolls. These are the traditional guardians of treasure in Indian legends. A simple kiosk adjoins this building, which is adorned by beautifully carved brackets, akin to those in Jain temples in western India. The use to which this kiosk was put remains a subject of speculation.

As he left the great courtyard towards the end of the day, Akbar may have felt the desire to enlighten himself in matters of religion. Controversy surrounds the site of the Ibadat Khana where the religious debates took place. Badauni tells us that in expectation of a visit by his uncle, 'a ruler with Sufic tendencies', the emperor ordered a cell formerly used by a *murid* (disciple) of Sheikh Salim Chishti, 'to be rebuilt and surrounded on all four sides by spacious *aiwans* (open verandahs). He named the cell Ibadat Khana.'

This hastily converted cell, which was the scene of much fierce debate, bad temper and recrimination, was possibly below the Jami Masjid. Originally intended for Muslim divines only, the gatherings were subsequently enlarged to include doctors of other faiths. To accommodate these larger gatherings, the Diwan-i-khas or the courtyard around Anup Talao were generally favoured, and the Ibadat Khana was abandoned. Because of the heresies associated with it, the converted cell might even have been surreptitiously demolished in subsequent reigns.

After the original Ibadat Khana was found inadequate,

Akbar seems to have preferred the more spacious area adjoining the Diwan-i-khas for religious discourses. This would lend support to the current official view that a series of open verandahs to the north-east of the Diwan-i-khas came to be used for the purpose. Indeed, the Diwan-i-khas itself is sometimes identified as the Ibadat Khana. However, even the most cursory glance at the perfectly proportioned Diwan-i-khas shows that it bears no resemblance to the converted cell described by Badauni. Some recent authorities have called it the Jewel House. Whether or not the Diwan-i-khas was actually used by Akbar as a store house for jewels, it is as perfect as a jewel casket, a masterpiece of the stone-cutter's craft. In the ten years they had been working for their patron, the *sang tarash* of Sikri had acquired a high measure of skill and refinement. But it is in the interior that their craft transcends the limitations of material. An elaborately carved stone capital, square at the base, then octagonal and finally sixteen-sided, springs upward from a setting in the centre, flaring into a cluster of fantastically carved brackets supporting an elevated seat. This in turn is connected to the four corners of the hall by low stone galleries, accessible from steep staircases on two sides.

The purpose of this beautiful structure remains a mystery. It could hardly have served as a hall for Akbar and his advisers, as some have suggested, with the emperor in the centre and ministers at the four ends, reading reports and taking orders. The column radiating to the four quarters could have been intended as a symbol. W.H. Siddiqui has suggested that it was a *satun-i-adl* (column of justice), from atop which Akbar announced important decisions. It could not have served any routine purpose. Akbar remained something of an enigma. None of his contemporaries were able to fathom the mystical depths of his mind. Today, we are left with indications, arrows that point though they may never pin the target.

Whatever the intention and purpose actually served, the execution and the structural devices of eaves, balustrades and brackets have a pronounced indigenous inspiration. The Diwan-i-khas is a perfect expression of the artistic syncretism that flourished under Akbar's patronage, just as he used his great authority to encourage tolerance of all faiths and to banish fanaticism.

Before he returned to his Khilwatkada-i-khas, Akbar }might have climbed the five storeys of the Panch Mahal, or Wind Tower, to refresh himself after the morning's activities and to survey the progress of construction in the city down below. After a rest, cushions would perhaps have been arranged in the small pavilion in the centre of Anup Talao. As the emperor settled down, Tan Sen would have been summoned to sing an evening *raga* as intricate as the carved decorations in the exquisite pavilion, or Hujra, close by. As the evening advanced, Akbar might have fancied a particular dance. The troop of *kanchanis* specially adept would glide past the columns, clashing the *ghungrus* on their ankles by turns, in spirited contention with the *tabalchi* (drummer).

In 1578, while hunting in the forests of Bhira in the Punjab, Akbar experienced a state of mystical exaltation. To everyone's astonishment, and his mother Mariam Makani's concern, the hunt was called off. On his return, Akbar had Anup Talao filled with coins of the value of 1.3 crore of rupees, so that 'the general public might receive an abundant share of the sublime bounty.' This enormous treasure consisted mostly of copper coins, but included gold and silver. Jahangir remarks that 'for a long time the thirsty-lipped ones of the desert of desire were satisfied from that fountain of benignity.'

Some of the finest carvings will be found in the pavilion adjoining Anup Talao. Floral designs alternate with arabesques with a fluency found only in the finest wood carvings. 'Clever workmen,' says Abul Fazl, 'chisel it so skilfully, as no turner could with wood; and their works vie with the picture book of Mani (the great painter of the Sassanides).' The interior is completely covered with carvings of pastoral scenes, with birds and animals appearing as if in their natural habitat.

There are striking representations of the tree of life motif. Siddiqui has established that Akbar received close friends and high dignitaries in this superbly elegant pavilion. Situated so close to Anup Talao and the emperor's Khilwatkada-i-khas, the suggestion that the pavilion was the residence of Ruqqayya Sultan Begum, Akbar's first wife, and Salima Sultan Begum, who he married later, strains belief. A mini seraglio within the emperor's personal area was a highly unlikely arrangement, more particularly as his *hammam* was next door. These beautifully lined stucco chambers provide insights to Akbar's personal habits. He is known to have been partial to scented oils; and he must have emerged from the succession of massage parlours and hot and cold baths, pummelled, scented and refreshed.

In keeping with Islamic tradition, the seraglio, or Haram Sara, is a distinct group of buildings. It is situated to the north-west of the emperors' palace, bounded by the road to the lake and Hiran Minar. In cultural terms, the seraglio is, perhaps, the most exciting part of Fatehpur. *Sehans* (courtyards), Hindu *chhajjas* (balconies), Gujarati architectural features, and decorative motifs derived from Hindu and Islamic traditions, all aptly blend and provide striking proof of the emergence of a genuinely syncretic Hindustani culture. This was indeed Akbar's greatest contribution to the development of Indian unity.

The seraglio's three main mahals were clearly intended for only the principal ladies. Closest of all to the emperor's Diwankhana-i-khas is Sunahra Makan, or Golden House. The Amber princess, who was given the name Mariam Zamani when she gave birth to the young prince Salim, is thought to have been the occupant. There is no question that as the mother of the heir apparent her position at court was virtually unassailable. South-west of it, and catching the morning sun, is the Shabistan-i-Iqbal, or principal Haram Sara, which was the residence of Akbar's other Hindu wives. At the western end is an architectural gem known as Birbal's house. A clear misnomer of course, for not even as one of Akbar's *nau ratna* (nine gems) could this imperial favourite and teller of droll stories have been given quarters in the most private of all the Haram Sara buildings. The mahal is a kind of duplex, with two sets of apartments. It was evidently designed for the convenience of the two most respected ladies, Akbar's mother, Mariam Makani, and his aunt, Gulbadan Begum, Babur's last surviving daughter. In this secluded corner, they were far removed from the comings and goings of visitors, serving maids and the noises from court and city. Close by is the small Nagina Masjid where these elderly ladies could conveniently observe their religious duties.

Sunahra Makan was evidently designed to suit Mariam Zamani's tastes. The plain exterior may now seem to belie the name, but Akbar's artists were encouraged to make a lavish display of their skills in the interior. The walls are painted with battle pictures, elephant fights and country idylls. Gold paint, from which the palace gets its name, was freely used. Unhappily, the paintings are now much faded, and the subjects cannot be positively identified, though the perspective appears to be Indian. Resourceful guides, who find it profitable to keep alive the myth propagated four hundred years ago by the Jesuits that Akbar was on the verge of embracing Christianity, are quick to improvise the interpretation that winged beings depicted in the paintings represent the Annunciation. In the Persian conception of the Queen of Sheba's visit to King Solomon winged female figures always occupy the centre of the composition. This could have been intended as an allegory for the Rajput princess' arrival in the court of an equally celebrated king.

Several Hindu motifs are used in the decorations, such as Hanuman worshipping Ram. Painted Persian inscriptions adorn the walls. One of the verses runs:

This building excels the seventh heaven in glory;
The excellence of the Kaba is beyond question, but this
mansion has a purity of its own.

Thus the mansion is exalted, but it is made clear beyond doubt that it cannot vie in excellence with the Kaba.

South-west of the Sunahra Makan is the Shabistan-i-iqbal, popularly knows as Jodha Bai's palace. With its guard-house adjoining the gate, and high walls sloping inwards in a distinct exterior batter, it seems to have been designed to create a sense of internal security. The impression of heavy solidity is relieved by a seemingly fortuitous, though cleverly contrived, arrangement of sandstone blocks of variegated colours. The middle course is lined with the interlocking tulip design characteristic of Fatehpur. Balustrated balconies break the surface monotony. There is a single baffle entrance, facing east, through a lintelled gateway flanked by elegant brackets, set within an arch fringed by a delicate row of cusps.

Once inside, the queens were in a world of their own. Apartments surround a spacious courtyard or *sehan*, distinctly Rajput in conception, and were not as cramped as the more famous Jahangiri Mahal in Agra fort. The Hindu princesses are believed to have freely observed their own religious practices, such as *havan*, in the courtyard and in their rooms.

The most striking external feature is the pair of blue-tiled rectangular roofs in the centre of the northern and southern sides. Glazed tiles were a Persian speciality, successfully developed in Multan and elsewhere in the Punjab. The tiles may have lost some of their original brilliance, but their survival, after over four hundred years of exposure to the harsh elements, is outstanding proof that the craft had been completely mastered. Set amongst the mortared domes and eaved kiosks breaking the morning skyline, the ribbed blue tiles of Jodha Bai's palace add a touch of variety that might have lost something of its uniqueness if Akbar had made liberal use of them elsewhere as well.

The Hawa Mahal, or Palace of Breezes, is a screened first-floor pavilion abutting from the Shabistan-i-iqbal. Royal ladies entered from within and could thence proceed by a screened passage, descending from level to level, to Hathi Pol Gate and the lake beyond. Screened on three sides, the pavilion may also have been one of Akbar's favourite resorts, but it seems more likely that he would have preferred the Panch Mahal, or Wind Tower, further to the north.

Deprived of most of its screens in an ill-advised attempt at modification in the 1870s and 80s, the five-storeyed Panch Mahal is a reminder of the grace and beauty it undoubtedly possessed in the days when Akbar climbed from storey to storey with his ladies. Overlooking the seraglio as it does, it is unlikely that any but the closest relatives were privileged to accompany him. The Wind Tower was Persian in conception but entirely Indian in execution. Each succeeding level was placed asymetrically and no two columns are exactly alike. Most of the motifs are Hindu in inspiration, which suggests that having told his builders what he wanted, Akbar left it to them to display their mastery of the art. It has been suggested elsewhere that Akbar created in Fatehpur a vast canvas, which he encouraged his workmen to fill with works of genius. Here, in the Panch Mahal, they responded nobly, creating, as Rizvi and Flynn say, 'a veritable museum of styles.'

107

The essential purpose was to create an ascending series of pavilions where the emperor could take his ease, cooled by breezes filtering through the screens which the British 'restorers' so thoughtlessly removed. Exciting views can be seen from the top, especially at dusk. The imagination must be allowed to fill in details of the lively scene, from the towering Buland Darwaza to the south and the lake to the north, adorned with Babur's pavilion. Peacocks would have been strutting on the rooftops as they do now, while groups of bejewelled courtiers awaited the emperor's return from his eyrie above. At nightfall, as Siddiqui suggests, the *akash diya* might have been lit and planted atop the Panch Mahal to illuminate the entire Daulat Khana and proclaim the emperor's presence.

How the palace known as Birbal's mahal came to be misnamed is a subject open to conjecture. It occupies the most prized situation in the whole of Fatehpur, and could only have been meant for the two senior ladies. There is no doubt, however, of the excellence of the architecture, the refinement of the decoration and the extraordinary technical skill of construction. E.W. Smith, whose great work is the earliest authoritative study of Fatehpur, has rightly called it the finest of the domestic buildings in the capital.

The delicacy of the carving of brackets, capitals and wall arabesques is particularly pleasing, and the ceilings of the ground floor rooms are designed with the elegance of lace. At first the perfection of the inner domed ceilings of the first floor may not be noticed, because the ribbed stone has been left uncarved. From the balconies, and even more so from the roof, the mahal commanded a splendid view of the lake. A further point of interest may be noticed: craftsmen's names are engraved in some of the capitals, and the *samvat* (Hindu lunar) year of 1629 (AD 1572) in one of the columns, along with the name 'Akbar Padshah.' Apparently the workman did this on his own, because the spellings are in a dialect.

Considering that the palace complex, the seraglio and some of the offices were occupied within a year or two, it is hardly surprising that some defects have been noticed, such as faulty alignment of the capitals in one of the rooms in Birbal's mahal. Akbar's enthusiasm may have been infectious, but he drove the workmen to the limits of endurance. The buildings, as Monserrate commented, 'have been built with extraordinary speed, by the help of a host of architects, masons and workmen. For instance, he built a very large peristyle surrounded with colonnades, two hundred feet (60.96 metres) square, in three months, and some circular baths three hundred feet, (91.44 metres) in circuit, with dressing rooms, private apartments and many water channels, in six months.' Flaws, like those that appear in handblock prints, were inevitable, but they are extremely rare.

Akbar seems to have left the tented camp and occupied an apartment in the Daulat Khana enclosure as soon as one was ready. He was in the thick of it. To save himself from the noise, says Monserrate, 'he had everything cleverly fashioned elsewhere, in accordance with the exact plan of the building, and then brought to the spot, and there fitted and fastened together.' Nothing is more inspiring than personal example. 'Zelaldinus,[4]' says Monserrate, 'is so devoted to building that he sometimes quarries himself along with other workmen. Nor does he shrink from watching, and even practising, for the sake of amusement, the craft of an ordinary artisan.' To suit him, a workshop was built near the palace, 'where also are studios and work rooms for the finer and more reputable arts, such as painting, goldsmith-work, tapestry-making, carpet and curtain-making, and the manufacture of arms.' This could have been none other than the workshop to the north-east of the palace complex.

For a Jesuit, whose sole concern was to win the emperor for the church of Christ, Monserrate's observations about the construction of Akbar's capital are of exceptional interest. The palaces, he says, 'are magnificently built, from foundation to cornice, of hewn stone, and are decorated both with painting and carving ... The roofs ... are not tiled, but are dome-shaped, protected from the weather from the outside by solid plaster covering the stone slabs. This forms a roof absolutely impervious to moisture. The palaces are decorated also with many pinnacles, supported on four columns, each of which forms a small covered portico.' Though domes were not unknown in domestic architecture, what makes some of these particularly noteworthy is that they are double domes, Birbal's mahal being a case in point. Already in vogue elsewhere in the Islamic world, double domes had also been used by Akbar's builders in Delhi in the tombs of Humayun and Atga Khan, and even earlier in the sixteenth century by the Lodis. Their purpose was to combine exterior proportion with internal convenience, while the space between served as insulation against heat.

Deserted, empty and greatly diminished in the four

hundred years since Akbar moved his court to Lahore, Fatehpur must be seen as much more than just a place that was built to be lived in. In Akbar's hands it became an immense stone picture frame in which all the arts of the time were given deliberate expression — the art of the stone-cutter, the painter, the immortal singer Tan Sen, the glittering *kanchanis* twirling through the stone columns, and the great master-builder, Akbar, at the centre of it all.

It was perhaps no more than a devotional impulse that took Akbar to Sikri, as it then was. Within a year, the saint in whose honour it was built expired in fulfilment of his own prophecy. Jahangir himself relates the supernatural event. Akbar, it seems, pressed the saint to reveal 'when he would depart to the abiding region.' Pointing to the infant, Salim, the saint said that when the prince would recite something from memory, 'this will be a sign of my union with God.' Strict orders were given that the prince was not to be taught to recite anything by heart. When he was two years and seven months of age, an old woman servant, in ignorance of this injunction, taught the young prince the opening lines of Jami's *Yusuf and Zulaikha:*

> *O God, open the rosebud of hope*
> *Display a flower from the everlasting garden.*

Salim went to the Sheikh and repeated the couplet. The saint was taken by fever the same night. He called the emperor, placed his turban on young Salim's head, saying: 'the promised time of union has come ...' He asked for Tan Sen to sing to him. Sheikh Salim's weakness increased until he attained fulfilment of the pious Sufi's longing for union with the 'True Beloved.'

In life, Akbar honoured him with a city. In death, he offered the tribute of an exquisite casket as a tomb. The child, whose recitation united the saint with God when he became the Emperor Jahangir, further embellished it with marble carvings of exceptional delicacy. A group of tombs towards the northern end of the great Jami Masjid courtyard provide a backdrop for the dazzling marble gem in the foreground. Originally executed in the red sandstone of Fatehpur, Jahangir's foster brother, Qutb-ud-din Khan Koka, veneered it completely with chaste white marble, and adorned the interior with painted decorations. The cenotaph lies below a graceful ebony catafalque, in which are embedded myriads of pieces of mother-o-pearl.

Beyond the tomb is the Jami Masjid, which is the real glory of Akbari architecture in Fatehpur Sikri. Built wholly in the arcuate style, it is one of the largest and finest mosques in India, remarkable for its ornamentation and rhythmical balance. Akbar would have entered through the Shahi Darwaza (Eastern Gate), closest to his Daulatkhana-i-khas, but the southern gate is the one he commissioned to celebrate his victory in Gujarat.

Buland Darwaza (Lofty Gate) is unquestionably the most majestic portal to any mosque in India. The aspect of loftiness is highlighted by a series of architectural devices in the exterior facade. The aspirant to the place of prayer within must first of all ascend a long flight of stairs, extending beyond the portal on either side. The effect of immensity is accentuated by thus arriving at the foot of the soaring arched recess. This is in the form of a half-decagon. Unlike other portals, the central face is flanked by wings sloping away towards the rear. The two side faces are broken into three stages of varied recesses, whose scale and treatment once again subtly emphasise the soaring height of the gateway. A message is proclaimed on the facade in beautiful lettering, 'Jesus, Son of Mary (on whom be peace), said: The world is a bride, pass over it but build no house upon it. Who hopes for an hour, hopes for eternity. The world is an hour. Spend it in prayer, for the rest is unseen.'

Inside, the portal is comparatively unpretentious. It descends in a series of levels, thus creating an impression of massive solidity. This again is totally deliberate, for the aim of the architect is to direct the worshipper to the house of prayer.

* * *

A question that tantalises the visitor even before he has set foot in Fatehpur, is why Akbar left. As already pointed out, he had to deal with a possible threat to the security of the empire from the north, but the story most often volunteered is that the city ran short of water. William Finch, who visited Fatehpur in the autumn of 1610 on his way to Bayana to buy *nill* (indigo) in one of the first English purchasing missions in the area, picked up an even more lurid story. 'Under the courtyard (of the mosque) is a goodly tanke of excellent water; none other being to be had through the citie, but brackish and fretting, by drinking whereof was caused such mortality that the Acubar, before it was quite finished left it, and removed his seat to Agra, so that this goodlie cite was short lived, in fifty or sixty years space being built and ruinate.'

113

The excellence of the water in the mosque is indisputable. The columns of the porch of the saint's tomb are hollow. Rainwater is drained from the roof, through the columns, to a small well in the south-eastern corner of the courtyard. The main well that supplied the imperial apartments is dry because the lake has been drained out, but there are still a number of sweet-water wells in Fatehpur and the old town of Sikri (sampled by the author without dire consequences). Behind the Daftar Khana is the Hakim's well, dating from Akbari time, which is still is use. Though not plentiful, drinking water was not really scarce. An engineering problem of this order was not beyond the immense resources of so determined an emperor as Akbar. 'To supply the city with water,' says Monserrate, 'a tank has been carefully and laboriously constructed, two miles long and a mile wide. The king descends to the lake on holidays, and refreshes himself with its many beauties.' The 'tank' was evidently the Sikri lake, which Akbar improved with thirteen new gates. The excellent Mr Finch is also in error about Akbar's departure to Agra, for it was to Lahore that the emperor went, not returning to Agra until 1598.

Even when the court had been in Fatehpur, Agra was never abandoned. Ralph Fitch, who visited the capital in the summer of 1585, was greatly impressed. 'Agra and Fatepore,' he says, 'are two very great cities, each of them much greater than London and very populous.' All the way between 'is a market of victuals and other things, as full as though a man was still in a towne, and so many people as if a man was in a market.' Fatehpur was indeed the cultural and administrative twin of Agra. It was not planned for defence, though the six kilometre city wall was provided with proforma defensive features. Agra fort remained the citadel and the repository of the imperial treasure while the emperor was in Fatehpur. But whether at Lahore or anywhere else, the imperial camp was always the capital. This was a relic from the nomadic Mughal past. Wherever he was, in the grandeur or Agra fort, or on the march by horse or camel, or even as a pilgrim journeying on foot to Hazrat Ajmer, or yet again, with splendid equipage on the great northern road planned and surveyed by his grandfather, the imperial capital was his camp, moving with him wherever he went.

Hardly forty years after Akbar's death, Shah Jahan was building another capital in Delhi. In 1681, Aurangzeb left the glittering palaces in both Delhi and Agra for the Deccan, from where he never returned. He, too, had imperial business, the twists of fate that were to seal the downfall of the great empire his ancestor had created.

---

1 Roughly from Chhata, north of Mathura, as far south as Agra and between the river Yamuna and the Aravalli hills.

2 Literally twelve doors but generally signifying a central chamber surrounded by verandahs or aiwans (open pavilions).

3 Virtually a cult group consisting of people who would neither wash nor eat, until they had been blessed by the auspicious presence of the emperor.

4 Jalal-ud-din, one of Akbar's names.

GENERAL PLAN OF FATEHPUR SIKRI

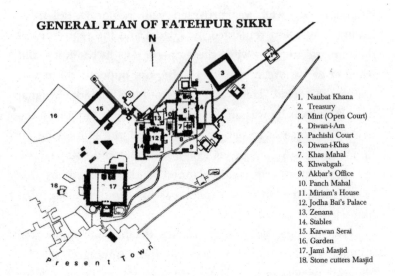

1. Naubat Khana
2. Treasury
3. Mint (Open Court)
4. Diwan-i-Am
5. Pachishi Court
6. Diwan-i-Khas
7. Khas Mahal
8. Khwabgah
9. Akbar's Office
10. Panch Mahal
11. Miriam's House
12. Jodha Bai's Palace
13. Zenana
14. Stables
15. Karwan Serai
16. Garden
17. Jami Masjid
18. Stone cutters Masjid

akbar's tomb: sikandra

Shah Jahan's self-confessed craze for marble, and his compulsive urge to build, deprived posterity, amongst other things, of Jahangir's pleasure pavilion in the fort. But for this gap, the fort would have presented the entire panorama of Mughal architecture. The evolution of style, from the manly strength of Akbar's red sandstone to Shah Jahan's decorated marbles, represents one of the most remarkable cultural developments of any age.

If the fort is an architectural panorama, Akbar's tomb is a single picture frame in which may be seen something even more extraordinary — the swift transformation from Akbar's distinctive style to the refined aestheticism of his son, Jahangir. This was possible because Akbar had made little headway with his own tomb, perhaps because some Indian astrologers had prophesied that he would live to be one hundred and twenty. Plans had been made and work started, but when Jahangir went there for the first time in 1608, three years after his father's death, he was distinctly disappointed.

Jahangir's visit was akin to a pilgrimage. 'If possible,' he says in his memoirs, 'I would walk on my head and (sweep the way) with my eyebrows; for my august father walked, in order to obtain an heir, namely me, on foot, from Fatehpur to Ajmer ... Hence, if I walk to my father's tomb, I shall after all not have done much.'

'When I entered,' he goes on, 'I saw no building over the tomb such as I would approve of, for I had expected to see an edifice which travellers would pronounce to be unrivalled in the world.' The architects, he adds, 'went on building after their taste ... They had been three or four years at work, when I ordered clever architects ... to build up several parts as I had before directed. Gradually a noble edifice arose, and a splendid garden was laid out round the mausoleum.'

Although he claims some credit for the 'noble edifice,' Jahangir did not presume to do more than 'build up several parts.' Most likely these additions were the garden and replacement of red sandstone by marble in the roof of the kiosks, and the dazzling cloister above. No one really knows. It is certain, however, that the unusual and exceptionally fine southern gateway is entirely Jahangiri. Thus, the conception and basic structure remain Akbari, while the embellishments were executed by his son.

Set in extensive grounds, now unhappily uncared for, attention is immediately arrested by the gateway to the walled *charbagh.* The central apse rises above the two *aiwans* (recesses) on either side, one above the other, and is surmounted by two finely proportioned oblong *chhattris*. Exquisite mosaics and inlays in coloured stones cover the exterior, while particularly happily designed arabesques adorn the spandrels. Conventional pilasters have been dispensed with. The skyline is broken instead by ornamental minarets, rising in perfect proportion from the four angles of the roof. They are unquestionably the gateway's crowning achievement. The tops of the *chhattris* were removed by the Jats when they occupied Agra in 1764, but have been competently restored. Although minarets became an accepted convention in subsequent Mughal architecture, the conception and treatment in the Sikandra gateway is entirely unique. Referred variations, with the minarets at the four corners of the monument, and then the terrace on which the monument stands, were introduced in quick succession in the tombs of Itimad-ud-Daula and Jahangir himself (in Lahore), and the incomparable Taj. The extraordinary compositional harmonies that can be derived from this single feature were demonstrated with exceptional skill in this great period of Mughal architecture.

In the centre of the grounds, and at the end of a long water-course, the monument rises through five different levels, each storey diminishing in size. Flanked by open verandahs, and decorated with sandstone kiosks topped with white marble, one has the sense of being lost in a maze. The open fifth floor, which forms the last step in the narrowing pyramid, is 21.34 square metres. It is girdled by a marble

119

cloister, enclosed by screens worked in beautiful geometric patterns.

From a distance, the whole structure gives the impression of being incomplete, like a pyramid without the top. Fergusson concluded that the platform in the centre of the top floor was designed to 'support a chamber crowned with a light dome ... The platform is supported on massive piers which would have been quite strong enough to support' such a feature. Finch, who visited Sikandra in 1611, is more positive. The tomb, he says, was meant 'to be inarched over with the most curious white and speckled marble, and to be seeled all within with pure sheet-gold, richly inwrought.' On his last visit to Sikandra, Finch says there was drawn over it 'a rich tent, with a semaine over the tombe.' Marble rings at the corners of the marble cloisters were evidently used to hold the 'rich tent' in place.

When visualised as 'inarched over with the most curious white and speckled marble,' the whole structure will be seen as complete, a kind of funerary counterpart to Akbar's five-storeyed Panch Mahal in Fatehpur. So unique that Fergusson surmised the design to be borrowed 'from a Hindu, or more correctly, Buddhist model,' it would be difficult to find any true parallel. Akbar, as we have seen, was his own architect in Fatehpur. Something so personal as his tomb is even more likely to embody his own ideas. The builders were able to continue work on the basis of the designs, until Jahangir made changes amounting to a decorative overlay. If indeed the top of the tomb was meant to be 'inarched over' with marble, Jahangir's omission could have been intentional. He may have left it open in compliance with his father's wishes, so that it could be covered with 'a rich tent' when *urs* were celebrated at the tomb.

As the visitor passes through the exceptionally striking entrance to the tomb and climbs through its four storeys to the top, the conviction grows that its creator was none other than the great emperor buried within. In conformity with convention, the sarcophagus, a plain white slab of marble, is in a sepulchre in the ground floor. Midway between the staircases on the south side of the fourth storey is a small aperture, through which it is possible to enter a low-roofed chamber where there is a false tomb. No one has been able to offer a convincing explanation of the purpose of this secret chamber.

With a sense of exhilaration the visitor at last reaches the open cloister at the top, a little more than 30.48 metres above ground level. From here splendid views may be had of the river Yamuna, the distant minarets of the Taj and, on clear days, Akbar's former capital on a ridge of the Aravalli hills. But attention is immediately taken up by the marble cenotaph in the centre of the cloister.

Adorned by the ninety names of Allah in delicate Arabic lettering, Akbar was consistent even in death, for there is no mention of the Prophet. From the very beginning of his reign he had emphasised the greatness of God which all men could acknowledge. Thus the phrase: 'Allah-hu-Akbar Jalla Jalalu-hu' (God is great, eminent is His glory) alone is inscribed on two faces of the marble cenotaph, the head and foot. Cloud forms also appear on these two panels. They have been attributed to

Chinese workmanship by those who forget that Chinese motifs were absorbed in the cultural matrix of Central Asia and brought to Hindustan, along with many others, from Persia. Indian workmen, who had no difficulty in making masterly depictions of the whole corpus, approached the task of representing cloud forms with their customary resolution and sureness of touch.

Before the visitor leaves, some time should be spared to study the care bestowed on irrigation systems in the garden, and what might be called the transition from Fatehpur's engraved red sandstone to the variegated marble mosaics of the great entrance gateway. Mughal architecture was clearly preparing to launch into another dimension, to the dream in marble eight kilometres downstream, of which the visitor caught a tantalising glimpse from the summit of Akbar's tomb.

Across the River

ARAM BAGH

'Then in that charmless and disorderly Hind, plots of garden were seen laid out with order and symmetry, with suitable borders and parterres in every corner, and in every border, rose and narcissus in perfect arrangement.'

Aram Bagh is believed to be Babur's original Gul Afshan garden, in which he sought relief from the heat of Agra and the cares of state. Seated somewhere in its cool avilions he dictated the literary gem of his memoirs. Though it is the first formal garden laid by the Mughals in Hindustan, and a protected monument, that distinction has not saved it from the consequences of total neglect. The garden is in an advanced state of dilapidation. The parterres, which Babur filled with flowers and fruits, including melons grown by a gardener the emperor brought from Balkh, are hardly distinguishable. The boundary walls are crumbling and inroads are being made by neighbouring factories and business premises.

The honeycombed corbels in the pavilions have been filled with painted figures, birds and flying ducks. Some of these figures are winged, suggesting Persian inspiration. Two half figures in the outer panels have Central Asian features and may thus be amongst the earliest Mughal paintings in Hindustan.

CHINI-KA-RAUZA

This *rauza* (tomb set in a garden), is unquestionably the finest funerary composition of glazed tile decoration in India. It is now much decayed, though enough has survived to suggest the singular beauty it possessed when Shukrulla Shirazi placed it alongside the river. In this respect the architects, or most likely Shukrulla himself in his lifetime, anticipated the ground plan of the Taj.

Shukrulla Shirazi was a scholar and poet in Persian. He had lived for many years in Lahore, where he must have fancied the glazed tiles for which Lahore and Multan were renowned. They had been used with great effect in a number of monuments and other buildings, such as the fort and Chauburji, in Lahore. Shukrulla became Dewan, or finance minister, to Shah Jahan, and seems to have built the tomb in which he and his wife were later buried. The *rauza* got its name from the porcelain tiles with which it is covered, and has nothing whatever to do with China.

Though conventional in plan, the architecture of this exquisite mausoleum is subordinated to the unrivalled display of tiles of fantastic design all over its surface. Thus the four outer faces are flat without any projecting eaves, courses and the like. Any consequent suggestion of monotony, however, is dispelled by the brilliance of the floral designs in variegated colours over the entire surface. Unhappily, large portions have been peeled off, with some assistance no doubt from passing vandals, and the dome tiles, arranged in geometric patterns, have almost completely disappeared.

The whole interior is covered with stucco, exquisitely painted with handsome floral and conventional designs. The soffit of the (double) dome is beautifully corbelled out into seven concentric honeycombed rings.

ITIMAD-UD-DAULA

Turning upstream after crossing the river, a rare experience awaits the visitor at the tomb of the Empress Nur Jahan's father, Mirza Ghyas Beg. Enslaved by the wiles and beauty of his Persian queen, Jahangir made the Mirza his prime minister in 1611, with the title of Itimad-ud-Daula (Reliance of the State). During his years in office, with the active support of his masterful daughter, the Persian faction gained an ascendancy at court, which provoked resentment amongst the Indian Muslims and Hindu nobility. While it lasted, however, Persian politesse, art styles and architectural conventions enjoyed unrivalled favour. Prevailing taste was expressed to perfection in the tomb built by the empress for her father after his death in 1621. It was completed in 1628, the year after Jahangir's death.

Jahangir was buried in Lahore, and Nur Jahan and her brother Asaf Khan were entombed near his mausoleum at Shahdara. Agra was chosen for Itimad-ud-Daula's mausoleum, probably because he had already, in his lifetime, constructed a *baradari* in the 164.60 metre square *charbagh* of which his tomb eventually became the centrepiece. The western gate of the high-walled *charbagh* is a riverside pavilion of great elegance and beauty. The festal hall that he had enjoyed in his lifetime was an appropriate choice for his last resting place. His wife Asmat Begum, who had died before him, was buried in the centre. When he followed, the great Persian nobleman was laid at her side, setting the pattern for the two graves in the Taj Mahal.

In other respects, too, the plan of the tomb closely follows convention. It occupies the central intersection of the *charbagh*, and the mortuary chamber is on the ground floor with a cenotaph chamber immediately above. In architectural terms, however, the tomb is not an entirely harmonious composition in the Persian tradition. The corner towers seem squat and the square dome surmounting the cenotaph chamber a trifle uncomfortable. There is also a suggestion of awkwardness in the attempt to incorporate certain indigenous features, such as corner kiosks and bracket-supported eaves and dripstones. The tomb of Itimad-ud-Daula marks a dramatic transition in Mughal architectural development, but it had yet to become a full-blown flower in Shah Jahan's nurturing hands.

Earlier, in the Akbari phase, the universal medium was red sandstone in relatively simple compositions, carved with unexampled exuberance. In the succeeding Shah Jahani phase with Jahangir taking the first decisive step towards a new aestheticism, an all-embracing veneer of white marble covered the entire structure, decorated by flowing and formal designs in mosaic or pietra dura inlay.

At its simplest, the change reflected the personalities of the two emperors, but also, and more deeply, the artistic evolution of the times. Transition from the deep lustrous tones of red sandstone was necessarily accompanied by adaptation of the harmonies of form and subtle use of decoration to suggest tonal qualities. Having chosen the medium of dazzling white marble, the architect of Itimad-ud-Daula's tomb was confronted by the problem of somehow moderating its excessive brilliance, and he did so by making use of the elusive tints of coloured stones embedded in its surface. The rhythmical harmonies of curvilinear form were less in evidence in this transitional phase. Only later were they triumphantly articulated by Shah Jahan.

The architect's decision to present the mausoleum as a jewelled casket, just 21.03 square metres, can be understood as his solution to the problems he faced. Though the whole ensemble seems a trifle earth-bound, he has succeeded in imparting an ethereal quality to it, by filling all possible spaces with lattices of exceptional beauty and an unrivalled display of decoration on every available surface.

Given this task, the decorators excelled themselves by profusely embellishing the marble with geometric and flowing designs, done in coloured marble mosaic and stone inlay. The sense of design and choice of colour never falters, and their harmonious combination is the real glory of Itimad-ud-Daula's tomb. An attempt may be made to describe just one detail, the floor decoration surrounding the cenotaphs. Starting from the four corners of the white marble floor, and surrounding the cenotaphs, is a leaf scroll in marble the colour of old gold, known as *khattu*. Large leaves, fashioned after Persian, Arabian and Turkish ornament, emerge at intervals from the concave sides of the leaf scroll. As a kind of subtle counterpoint, an intricate design in bluish black stone underlies the leaf scroll, while leaves and flowers of variegated *abri* (jasper) emerge from its meanders.

The flowing designs in the floor are set off by walls displaying a combination of scrolls, geometric designs, representations of cypresses, cups, decanters and *guldastas* (flower vases) distinctly Persian in inspiration, and beautiful friezes in Naskh characters above the arches. The soffits frame incised carvings of matchless delicacy. Thus the decorations, starting from the floor, are taken over by the dados to merge finally in the roof. Such range and variety as the designers presented in this small gem are altogether unique.

taj mahal

'The Lady of the Taj', was one of the three remarkable imperial consorts who created an imperishable niche for themselves in the history of the Mughal empire. All three were Persian. The first was Hamida Bano Begum, who, when barely fifteen, was married to Humayun in the wilds of Sind, and sustained the fugitive emperor with the solace of her companionship during his fifteen year exile. The second was Nur Jahan, whose intelligence and renowned beauty so enslaved Jahangir that he virtually committed the empire to her care. The last of the three was Arjumand Bano Begum, who was given the name Mumtaz Mahal. Her devotion to her husband, the Emperor Shah Jahan, inspired the finest mausoleum ever to be created by man.

As soon as Jahangir married Nur Jahan in 1611, she deftly insinuated her close relations into the highest offices in the realm, and arranged marriages aimed at ensuring their hold on power. Her father, Itimad-ud-Daula, was appointed Prime Minister, an office he held until his death in 1621. Her daughter by her first husband, Sher Afghan, was married to the emperor's youngest son, Shahryar. But what turned out to be a much more auspicious match was the marriage in 1612 of her brother Asaf Khan's daughter, Arjumand Bano Begum, with Prince Khurram. Although Jahangir had not appointed him heir apparent, after Khusro's rebellion and blinding, Khurram's claims to the succession could not be brushed aside. When Jahangir died in 1627, Nur Jahan's attempt to finesse the succession in favour of Shahryar was checkmated by her own brother. Asaf Khan moved swiftly. In one of the bloodiest successions in Mughal history, Khurram's rivals were eliminated and the prince was proclaimed emperor in 1628 with the title of Shah Jahan.

Though Shah Jahan had been married to a descendant of Shah Ismail of Persia two years before he married Mumtaz Mahal, and later contracted a 'political' alliance with the granddaughter of Abdur Rahim *Khan-i-Khanan*, Mumtaz was his unquestioned favourite. She in turn proved her devotion by accompanying him wherever he went. Soon after his accession, Shah Jahan marched southwards to deal with Khan Jahan Lodi's rebellion in the Deccan. The empress went with him; the two were inseparable.

While the emperor was encamped at Burhanpur, the empress died giving birth to her fourteenth child. Her last hours have been described by Mulla Abdul Hamid Lahori in the *Badshah Nama* and Muhammad Saleh in his *Amal-i-Saleh*. Knowing that her end was near, the empress sent her eldest daughter, Jahanara, to call the emperor. She entreated Shah Jahan to take good care of their children after she had left this world. He was stricken with grief, and on 28 June, 1631, she died while he gazed into her fading eyes.

According to the *Badshah Nama*, Shah Jahan's beard, which had been streaked by just a few grey hairs, became almost completely white during his emotional ordeal. Every Friday he visited the temporary grave in the garden of Zinabad in Burhanpur. For two years the emperor completely abstained from rich food, wore the simplest clothes, and banned musical entertainments and other celebrations. Muhammad Saleh tells us that mourning was observed by the court for the whole month of *Zika-ad* for several years thereafter.

Six months after the empress' death, her body was taken to Agra by Prince Shuja, the court physician Wazir Khan and Sati-un-nisa Khanam, Mumtaz Mahals' favourite maid servant. The cortege arrived there on 9 February 1632. Detained by affairs in the Deccan, the emperor himself could not return to Agra until 10 June. The coffin had been laid in a temporary grave in the garden of Raja Jai Singh of Amber, who had inherited it from his grandfather, Akbar's celebrated general, Raja Man Singh. It was here that Shah Jahan decided to build a fitting *rauza* for the deceased empress. According to a *farman* of 18 December 1633, the emperor gave Raja Jai Singh four *havelis* (mansions) that were *khalsa* (crown) property as compensation for the garden.

Shah Jahan had returned to Agra just in time for Mumtaz Mahal's first death anniversary. According to the *Badshah Nama,* a grand feast was given by the emperor on the occasion, presumably near her temporary resting place. Superb tents and costly *shamianas* were put up. Princes of the blood and the leading amirs were in attendance. Learned *ulama*, sheikhs and *huffaz* (those who recite the Quran from memory) were also present. Places were allotted in the *shamiana* according to rank, and the emperor himself seated Asaf Khan, the late empress' father, next to Muhammad Ali Beg, the Persian ambassador. A magnificent dinner was served, consisting of a variety of delicious dishes, sweetmeats and fruits. Verses from the Quran were read and prayers offered for the soul of the deceased empress. Fifty thousand rupees were distributed in charity on the occasion, and an equal amount the following day. In subsequent years, a similar sum was distributed when the emperor was in Akbarabad, and twelve thousand rupees if he was away. The poor were fed in the cloisters near the main entrance.

A woman who dies in childbirth was considered a *shaheed* (martyr) and her tomb an *urs* (place of pilgrimage). Thus, the completion of the mausoleum was celebrated in a fitting manner. According to the *Amal-i-Saleh*, Sheikh Abdus Samad Amudi, who had come from Mecca, conducted the solemn ceremonies. Prayers were said, and recitations from the Quran were repeated constantly in the halls surrounding the cenotaph chamber, an observance that continues to this day.

Shah Jahan the Magnificent, who had created the Taj Mahal over the remains of his devoted wife and constant companion, followed her to the grave after his death on February 1666, (26 Rajab, AH 1076). In life he used to sail down the river by barge to the mausoleum. His last journey also was downstream. Mulla Abdul Hamid Lahori tells us that when the deposed emperor died in the fort, his body was brought from Samman Burj to the Diwan-i-khas, and from there taken down to the river through the water gate. The cortege sailed solemnly to the pier below the royal entrance to the tomb. The coffin was raised on the shoulders of his loyal followers and laid to rest in the vault on Mumtaz Mahal's right.

In keeping with convention, the actual graves were in the ground, while memorial cenotaphs were replicated in the vaulted chamber directly above. The empress' body was in the centre and her husband's beside hers, exactly reproducing the earlier arrangement in Itmad-ud-Daula's tomb. Emperor and queen, who had never left each other in life, rest together forever in the tomb he built in Akbarabad.

The Taj Mahal incomparably serves its purpose of being a tomb, but it is very much more than that. As Fergusson points out, 'during the lifetime of the founder, the central building is called a *baradari*, or "festal hall", and is used as a place of recreation and feasting by him and his friends. After his death the purpose is changed; he is interred beneath the central dome and sometimes his favourite wife lies beside him.' Tomb, festal hall, place of pilgrimage, worship, of annual celebrations and restrained enjoyment, Shah Jahan is unlikely to have planned another burial place for himself. If at all he did, only his daughter Jahanara, who remained with him to the end, could have left the secret to posterity. He could hardly have wished a happier fate than to lie beside his devoted wife in his most beautiful creation.

* * *

The choice of Raja Jai Singh's garden as the site for the *rauza* was itself an artistic decision. The whole strand of over a kilometre from the fort was taken up by gardens and pavilions belonging to the nobility. Closest to the citadel was Asaf Khan's magnificent palace. Further on there were others, including Raja Todar Mal's *baradari*, rather similar, it must be supposed, to his residence in Fatehpur, now in ruins. Shah Jahan would readily have been given any of these, but he chose the last before the river turns slightly south eastwards. Seen from the Samman Burj in Agra fort, it will be appreciated at once as the finest view in the whole strand.

It was clear from this decision that Shah Jahan planned a riverside *rauza*. What he wanted to see from Samman Burj was the tomb itself and not the northern wall and false gateways characteristic of a *charbagh*, or even a riverside pavilion, as in Itimad-ud-Daula's tomb. The finest talent in his empire was assembled and the whole stupendous undertaking, we are told in the *Badshah Nama*, was placed under the superintendence of Abdul Karim and Makramat Khan, two high ranking *mansabdars*.

Neither of the two principal contemporary authorities mention an architect. In fact there could not have been a single architect solely responsible for the Taj, in the way that Wren was the architect of St Paul's in London. Mughal traditions were entirely different. The chroniclers mentioned only the high ranking nobles whom the emperors appointed to supervise construction. Individual artists and craftsmen sometimes painted or inscribed their names on their own works, as was the practice of the artists of the imperial atelier. In the Taj itself, the calligraphist of the Persian inscription on the entrance has inscribed his name at the end. In great architectural works, created by teams of designers, builders and master craftsmen, individual claims of this nature would have been completely out of place.

Nevertheless, there was known to be a practice of appointing a *mimar-i-kul* (chief architect), whose function would have been to coordinate the work of all the designers and produce the approved plan. Contemporary epigraphic and historical evidence establishes beyond doubt that Ustad Ahmad Lahori was Shah Jahan's *mimar-i-kul*. An inscription on his grave at Aurangabad tells us that he was the builder of the Taj in Agra, and the fort and Jami Masjid in Delhi. This claim is repeated in his son Lutfullah's *masnavi*, a work completed in 1655-56 (AH 1066) when Shah Jahan was still on the throne. Ustad Ahmad's eldest son, Ataullah Rashidi, in his contemporary chronicle, *Khulasat-ul-Hisab*, names his father as the *mimar-i-kul* of the emperor, Shah Jahan. This impressive contemporary evidence stands unrefuted.

The tradition that Shah Jahan set up a kind of board of experts who had a wooden model prepared, is in no way inconsistent with the claims of Ustad Ahmad's sons that their father was Shah Jahan's *mimar-i-kul*. The great works of Mughal architecture were essentially imperial in inspiration and scale. The emperor would have had to be served by a wealth of talent, coordinated by his *mimar-*

i-kul, all working under the superintendence of a high ranking amir.

The Mughal emperors were men of unusually good taste, and abundantly blessed with the means of giving expression to their individual visions of the beautiful. Shah Jahan's forte was the perfection of architectural form and excellence of decoration. While competent persons were entrusted with the practical tasks, there seems little doubt that the inspiration for the Taj was essentially his own. A verse composed by Shah Jahan, and inscribed on the tomb, includes the revealing lines.

The builder could not have been of this earth,
For it is evident the design was given him by heaven.

Though Persian poetry is replete with graceful refinements, the recipient of this heavenly inspiration could have been no one but the emperor himself. Ustad Ahmad and his associates were the agency through whom Shah Jahan gave form to the design 'given him by heaven.'

The *ustad* (master) was typical of the outstanding Muslim architects and perfectionist Hindu craftsmen who together produced the masterpieces of Mughal architecture. The Taj represents the culmination of an essentially Indian synthesis. In architectural terms the predominant strand is unquestionably Persian, but the synthesis is so complete, so utterly harmonious that any attempt to isolate one strand from the other would be meaningless.

* * *

More stories, apocryphal and true, have been inspired by the Taj Mahal than any other monument in India. Some of these

136

have been absorbed in the literature of the Taj and should be considered before going any further. Hardest to die was the myth, avidly taken up in the West, that the architect was the Venetian Geronimo Veroneo. European authors gave it a decent burial, when irrefutable evidence became available that the story propagated by Father Manrique following a visit to Agra in 1640 was at best a fine effort of imagination. Veroneo, who was a jeweller, had died in Lahore earlier in the year, and was buried in Agra. His unpretentious gravestone makes no such claim. Mundy, Tavernier and others, who were in Agra while the Taj was being built, or soon afterwards, never mentioned Veroneo as the architect, or anyone else for that matter.

Currency was then given to the attribution to Isa Muhammad Effendi, an architect reputedly sent by the Sultan of Turkey. Albeit from the Islamic world, Effendi was still not a Hindustani. This bold claim was made in a Persian manuscript of 1878 by Mughal Beg entitled *Tarikh-i-Taj Mahal*, now in the Taj museum. Though the author claims that his manuscript was based on earlier works, these are not specified. Established authorities regard the manuscript with undisguised suspicion. It was written at a time when foreign art historians had convinced themselves that the best in Mughal architecture was Saracenic in inspiration. The term itself raised the question of what Saracenic was. A number of copies of the manuscript were made, and there are grounds for believing that Mughal Beg was encouraged in his enterprise by the foreign principal of a local college. The claim that Isa Muhammad Effendi was the architect lacks any contemporary authority or corroboration, and must be viewed as untenable in the light of the positive evidence pointing to Ustad Ahmad Lahori.

Credulity and the Western obsession with establishing the identity of a supposed architect was taken to even more absurd lengths. Sleeman, who had been in India since 1810, confidently asserted in his *Rambles and Recollections*, published in 1844, that the Taj and the palaces in Agra and Delhi had been designed by Austin de Bordeaux, 'a Frenchman of great talent and merit, in whose ability and integrity, the emperor placed much reliance.' Austin, a jeweller, is known to have been making a living by his wits in Agra during the early years of Shah Jahan's reign. He died in 1632, while work on the Taj commenced after the emperor's return to Agra in June that year. Not to be outdone, he was then credited with creation of a gem-encrusted solid gold rail around the empress' cenotaph in the Taj. The cenotaph was not laced in position until 1636 and there was no question of enclosing it until long after the Frenchman had died. Peter Mundy's claim that there was already about her tomb 'a rail of gold' (in 1632) can only refer to the temporary grave.

A tale so picturesque that one might be tempted to allow it to stand has found its way into the literature of the Taj. Mughal Beg's was not the only manuscript to mysteriously appear in the middle of the nineteenth century. The first edition of *Guide to the Taj in Agra* was published in 1854 under the initials J.T.N. A subsequent edition was published in Lahore in 1862, It claims to have been based on an unnamed Persian manuscript, which relates the most touching of all the stories connected with the Taj. The Empress Mumtaz Mahal, who was *enceinte*, heard her unborn child cry out while still in her womb. 'When a child cries before its birth,' she confided to the emperor, 'the mother always dies; therefore I must prepare to take leave of this world.' She made him promise never to remarry and to 'build over me such a beautiful tomb as the world never saw'.

There is no mention of this tragic tale in the *Badshah Nama* and *Amal-i-Saleh*. Contemporary chroniclers were never loathe to allude to the miraculous and supernatural. The silence of the two authoritative biographers suggests, at any rate, that they never heard of it. Nevertheless, though he survived Mumtaz Mahal by twenty-five years, Shah Jahan never took another wife, and no one will dispute that his monument to the 'Light of the Palace' far exceeds in beauty, any other tomb ever made.

The French jeweller, Jean-Baptiste Tavernier, relates yet another story which has proved much more enduring than most. 'Shah Jahan,' he says, 'began to build his own tomb on the other side of the river, but the war with his sons interrupted the plan and Aurangzeb, who reigns at present, is not disposed to complete it.' A surprising statement, because there was nothing to complete. Tavernier was in India in 1640-41 and again for two months in 1665, thirteen years after the last stone had been laid in the forecourt and nearly twenty after the Taj itself was complete. Shah Jahan had ample time for this vainglorious enterprise, if he ever seriously intended it, before he was imprisoned by Aurangzeb. Neither Mulla Abdul Hamid Lahori nor Muhammad Saleh breathe a word about a second mausoleum. The truth is that Shah Jahan's attention had been diverted to Delhi, where he started building Shahjahanabad in 1638, ten years before the Taj itself was complete.

Mehtab Burj, across the river, which some writers have picked on as evidence of a start, with whoops of joy normally reserved for discoveries of bone fragments of the earliest homo sapiens, is nothing more than the last remaining vestige of one of the gardens made in Babur's reign. The *burj* (tower) is hardly 3.66 metres in height as against 13.11 metres of the riverside towers of the Taj. Remains of Humayun's masjid are a little further off. Whatever Shah Jahan's intentions might have been, good sense, no less than taste, spared posterity a rival to the Taj.

* * *

Shah Jahan seems to have lost no time in starting work on the Taj after his return from the Deccan in June 1632 and observance of the empress' first death anniversary. The scene is set in the Samman Burj in Agra fort. The emperor, seated on his gem-studded *awrang* (throne), leans forward and points to the site along the river. He brushes the architects aside, as he tells them what he sees filling the vacant space. 'Karamat! Karamat!' they exclaim, as they back away and get to work again. At last it comes right on the drawing boards. Models are prepared, and one of these may have been kept in the emperor's Daulatkhana-i-khas to refer to, from time to time.

When work started in 1632, the finest workmen and builders flocked to Agra from all over Hindustan and West Asia. According to the *Badshah Nama*, Ismail Khan of Turkey built the two-shell dome. A number of similar particulars have been given in the *Guide to the Taj in Agra*, published in Lahore, and Mughal Beg's manuscript of 1878. Some of this information, which is not specially controversial, may be of interest. The *Tarikh-i-Taj Mahal* ascribes the passages from the Quran, inscribed in Naskh characters on different parts of the monument, to the celebrated calligraphist, Amanat Khan Shirazi. The mastermason was Muhammad Hanif from Baghdad, who was paid Rs 1,000 a month. Kayam Khan, pinnacle maker, who was from Lahore, was paid Rs 695. There were a great many others for various kinds of work from Delhi, Cuttack, Punjab and Persia, on salaries ranging from Rs 100 to 500. Mughal Beg's statement that Mannu Beg of Turkey was the chief *pachikar* (mosaic worker), has been put seriously in doubt by records found by Havell in the Imperial (now National) Library in Calcutta. These records give a list of five principal mosaic workers, all of them Hindus. Mughal Beg could hardly have been wrong about the calligraphist of the inscription on the entrance of the tomb because the artist's name appears at the end of the inscription itself.

The *Badshah Nama* of Abdul Hamid Lahori puts the cost of the completed monument at Rs 50 lakh. Nevertheless, the manuscript on which the *Guide* published in Lahore is based enabled the author to claim that Indian rulers contributed Rs 98,55,426, while the imperial treasury made payments amounting to Rs 86,09,760. Sleeman was told in 1836, apparently by the *khadims* (caretakers), that the cost was Rs 3,17,48,026 or £3,174,802 sterling at the time. The very precision of these two conflicting figures, compiled two hundred years later, suggests that they were largely conjectural. The true total cost cannot be accurately computed. No detailed accounts have been preserved. The recorded expenditure of Rs 50 lakh as given in the *Badshah Nama*, may indicate the amount expended on miscellaneous petty charges and the wages of the 20,000 workmen who laboured for twenty-two years.

We are not told how the cost of the Taj was met, or whether a special levy was raised, as in the case of Agra fort. The empire, it must be remembered, had been at peace since Akbar's death, except for an occasional campaign in the Deccan. The total cost was not beyond the enormous accumulated resources of the treasury, even if it ranged between three and six crore rupees, as is thought by some authorities.

In accordance with custom, when granted the privilege of audience with the emperor, visiting dignitaries invariably offered *nazrana*. There is no warrant for the suggestion that special contributions were invited for the Taj. On the other hand, two *farmans* of Shah Jahan in the Bikaner archives, addressed to Raja Jai Singh of Amber, have recently come to light which clearly indicate the procedure adopted for procuring marble from the Makrana mines. Purchases were made and the charges regularly paid from the imperial treasury through Ilahdad Khan and Muluk Shah, two special officers posted there for the purpose. This information contradicts the popular belief that marble was supplied by vassal states without payment.[1]

It should be remembered, too, that the Mughal emperors dealt firmly with official oppression. When complaints were made to Shah Jahan by workers in the saffron plantations in Kashmir against imperial officials, the guilty were promptly punished. Although arrangements for payment to workers at the Taj could not have been proof against rapacious officials, discontent on this account has not been mentioned even in the accounts of the numerous foreign visitors. The doggerel circulating at the time:

Have mercy, God, on our distress.
For we, too, are with the princess,

was no more than the kind of fun versifiers made in such situations.

The *Tarikh-i-Taj Mahal* gives the places of origin and cost of some of the materials used. Yellow Marble, at Rs. 40 per square Shah Jahani yard, was from the banks of the Narbada river in central India and black from Charkoh (Four Hills) at Rs 90. White marble came from Jaipur, cost not being specified. Crystal was from China at Rs 570 and lapis lazuli from Lanka at Rs 1,156. A list of stones follows: jasper from the Punjab, carnelian from Baghdad, turquoise from Tibet, agate from the Yemen, coral from Arabia and the Red Sea, garnets from Bundelkhand and diamonds from Jaisalmer, rockspar from the Narbada, loadstone from Gwalior, onyx from Persia and chalcedony from *Wilayat* (Europe). Amethysts were from Persia and sapphires from Lanka. From nearby Fatehpur Sikri 1,14,000 cartloads of sandstone are said to have been brought. The sources of all these precious and semiprecious stones and other materials have not changed in the last 350 years.

An immense amount of labour was necessary for carting materials, dressing the stone at site, cutting and chiselling the precious stones to be inlaid in marble, mixing mortar and heaving marble slabs, stones and other material into position. Judging from the large number of depressions and mounds in the neighbourhood, the small burnt bricks measuring 16.5 x 11.5 x 3.8 cms were made as close to the site as possible. Jacob's Castle, now in ruins, stands on one of these mounds. When Manrique visited Bayana in 1640 before he died, he came across blocks of marble being carted to Agra. Some of these, he says, 'were of such unusual size and length that they drew the sweat of many powerful teams of oxen and of fierce-looking, big-horned buffaloes, which were dragging enormous, strongly made wagons, in teams of twenty or thirty animals.'

It has been calculated that the walls of the cenotaph chamber carry a massive load of 7.9 tons (8.02 metric) per square foot, while the dome, as it rests on its drum, weighs 12,000 tons (12,192.56 metric). The massive weight of the monument rests on arched vaults supported by a series of bricklined wells sunk below the plinth. Rubble and hydraulic lime were rammed into the wells, forming a solid foundation resting on the bedrock below. Poles of *sal* (*Shorea robusta*) were bound together with iron bands, riveted with copper bolts; these were then piled upright atop the lime masonry base. The core of each well was filled with rubble bonded with mortar, and the spaces between were rammed with stone and lime. Similar wells were sunk in the sand along the river-front of the Taj to protect it from erosion and floods. Although such well foundations had been used by Mughal builders in other monuments along the river, the construction of the Taj is clearly an engineering achievement of stupendous magnitude, even in the context of present-day knowledge.

It could hardly be sheer accident that the river Yamuna flows majestically due west to east past the monument. Indeed, there is a persistent tradition that it was slightly diverted to bring it alongside. There are no visible signs now of diversionary works, but a series of masonry embankments all the way from Balkeshwar mandir, about a kilometre upstream from Aram Bagh, serve the same purpose. Seemingly, the effect is to direct the river towards the knotch below the Agra fort, from where it turns eastwards. From this point the flow exactly corresponds to the orientations of the ground plan, an arrangement that provides views ranging from the majestic to the ethereal. From the opposite bank, on a misty morning, the Taj is transported into the air like a fairy castle floating in gossamer.

It would have been entirely in keeping with the comprehensive planning that went into the creation of this masterpiece, that Shah Jahan's unknown engineers triumphantly met the challenge of creating a permanent river front for a monument designed for such a setting. Ali Mardan Khan, *Amir-ul-Umara*, is known to have been living in Agra towards the end of the decade. This Persian engineering genius, who directed the construction of the original Lahore canal, could not have found such a diversion beyond his competence.

145

With the entire structure enclosed in a sheath of brick scaffolding, the builders must have had to rely almost completely on previously prepared plans and models. One of the original drawings of the Taj was last seen in 1916 in the possession of one Sharaf-ud-din, whose ancestor was an architect in Shah Jahan's service. This missing document could hold the key to some of the still unresolved mysteries of the Taj.

An aura of mystery has been created by a suggestion that the bodies might actually have been laid in the sealed chambers below the basement. The explanation is quite simple. These chambers were closed as a measure of protection against possible damage. When Aurangzeb was in Agra before the war of succession, he reported signs of damage to Shah Jahan, who was in Delhi. The emperor directed his son to carry out necessary repairs, and this was done. Although there is no positive evidence, it is possible that the chambers were sealed in the course of these protective works, for the masonry is Shah Jahani. A great deal is known about the Taj, but it is perhaps fitting that some of the secrets of its elusive beauty should remain unresolved.

Tavernier's statement that twenty-two years had been spent on the 'accomplishment of this great work' is confirmed by inscriptions on various parts of the monument. The year AH 1047 appears on the western facade of the mausoleum and AH 1048 on the southern wall of the cenotaph chamber, corresponding to AD 1637 and 1639. The Arabic inscription: 'The end with the help of God', appearing on the northern face of the main gateway, reveals that the entire monument, with the exception of the forecourt, was completed in AD 1648

(AH 1057). The forecourt and its ancillaries took another five years, or twenty-two years in all.

Tavernier also heard 'that the scaffoldings alone cost more than the entire work, because, from want of wood, they as well as the supports of the arches, had all to be made of brick; this had entailed much labour and heavy expenditure.' The story goes that Shah Jahan solved the problem of dismantling the scaffoldings, by letting it be known that the people who removed the bricks could keep them. The whole thing vanished with electrifying speed. At last the Taj Mahal stood fully revealed in the design given to Shah Jahan by heaven.

* * *

While planning the Taj Mahal, the *mimar-i-kul* necessarily had to take account of its character both as a *rauza* and an *urs*. If it had been nothing more than a *rauza*, a tomb set in a garden would have sufficed. But since it was also a place of pilgrimage, to be visited by thousands of people from far and near, functional provision had also to be made for the ceremonies connected with the anniversaries of the empress' death. Pilgrims would need a place to stay in and the poor an area where they could receive alms, food and clothes. The large establishment attached to the monument needed a shopping centre of its own, even though the bustling township of Tajganj, known as Mumtazabad at the time, had the customary commodity bazaars. Above all, the architect had to find a place of honour for the mosque. Ustad Ahmad Lahori adopted a simple layout to meet all these requirements.

147

A large rectangular area, roughly 579.12 metres long and 304.80 metres broad, was measured out in Raja Jai Singh's garden, from the riverside at the northern end up to the present day *qasba* of Tajganj. It was divided into two unequal portions. A small rectangle about 137.16 metres broad adjoining the *qasba* was set apart for a forecourt. This was completely enclosed and provided with entrances on three sides and a gateway to the *rauza* in the middle of the northern wall. The *charbagh*, mosque and tomb were placed in the larger portion, ending in an open platform and raised terrace overlooking the river. It was on this terrace that the *mimar-i-kul* placed the mausoleum in obedience to the emperor's wishes. Walls enclosed the other three sides. This was the true *rauza*. A lofty gateway at the southern end was the only public entrance. For the emperor and his closest companions arriving by barge, a passage was provided from the embankment direct to the terrace and thence to the tomb. This is now closed.

Additions, not directly related to the Taj Mahal had to be made later to accommodate the tombs of the empress' *sahelis*, or close companions. The devoted Sati-un-nisa Khanam was buried in a corner of the forecourt, while Fatehpuri Begum's tomb is to the left of the western entrance, with a mosque bearing her name alongside the southern end of the western wall. Sarhindi Begum, and Akbarabadi Begum, the emperor's two other wives, were buried outside the eastern entrance.

Inside the forecourt are the Jilau Khana, or large bazaar with cloisters, and the Khwaspuras or servants' quarters, at the north-eastern and north-western corners. The western entrance

148

to the forecourt is now the one mostly in use, but the enterprising visitor will find the southern entrance through the old satellite *qasba* of Tajganj a refreshing change. He will immediately be struck by the sheer grandeur of the main gateway to the Taj Mahal. Built in red sandstone, the structure conveys an impression of great strength, relieved by the beauty of its marble facings and exceptionally striking spandrels.

The three-storeyed gateway, set in the northern wall of the forecourt, is a magnificent example of Persian design. An imposing central *aiwan* (apsed entrance) flanked on either side by apsed recesses, one above the other, ends in robust octagonal corner towers, topped by matching *chhattris*. A coronal of entrancing elegance breaks the skyline. It consists of a narrow drip-stoned gallery, faced on each side by a cusped arcade of eleven bays surmounted by a similar number of small cupolas. Slender minarets, Persian in conception, rise along the quoins on either side to burst in fluted finials above the coronal. The southern facade is repeated on the northern side facing the tomb. The apsed entrances, front and back, are framed with marble bands, inscribed in black slate with Quranic texts, the letters being fashioned so that they appear to be of uniform size.

The doors set in the recessed entrance were originally of silver, studded with 100 silver rupees. These were looted by the Jats when they sacked Agra in 1764 and melted down, so that they are lost forever. The gateway opens into an octagonal chamber rising to a lofty domed vault, decorated with a network of designs in white stucco on a red background. Red and white stucco meticulously incised also decorates

149

the vaults of the mosque and Mihman Khana flanking the tomb.

Emerging from the gateway, the tomb stands fully revealed, perhaps a shade too explicitly. This is because the present garden is very different from the *charbagh* laid by Shah Jahan, not in form but in plant material. There were no lawns as such. It was a mixed garden of flowers and cypresses along the watercourses, rising in height towards the outer walls with flowering shrubs, fruit and flowering trees of moderate height, and finally mangoes and even the towering *imli* (tamarind). The flowers were the varieties favoured by the Mughals, especially narcissi, fritillaries, crocuses, irises, and the tulips from the Paghman range beyond Kabul which had so fascinated Babur. Dahlias, which were much admired by Akbar, were planted in masses. A wealth of flowering shrubs were grouped on the sides, such as jasmins of various kinds, a quamoclit with the Persian name of *Isq pechan*, and *Mirabilis jalapa*, known as the flower of Abbas. Next were *Plumeria alba*, the two *mimusops* (*elengii* and *hexandra*) and the Persian lilac, commonly known in Hindustan by the humbler name of *bakain*. Three kinds of palms were grouped in various corners. There were as many as five varieties of fruits — two citrus, pomegranates, guavas, *sharifa* (anona squamosa) and the inevitable mango. Jahangir declared that the mango was his favourite fruit. Consignments of the Alphonso variety were sent for the imperial table all the way from Goa.

Several of the flowers grown in the *charbagh* are depicted in the reliefs and inlays in the mausoleum, but the only one shown in its entirety is the toddy palm. The interested visitor

A carved floral panel on sandstone adorning the mosque on the left of the Taj.

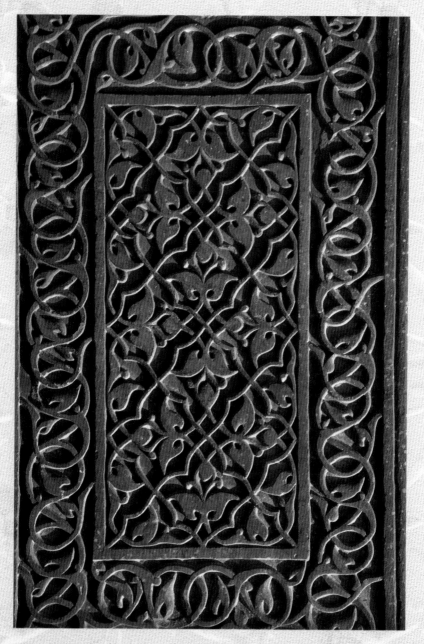

The decorations on the Taj represent the many flowers that were planted in the gardens.

Details of carvings on sandstone from the mosque in the Taj Mahal complex. The consummate artistry of the builders combined the Hindu love for decoration with the Persianised designs to create an effect that was rich. The sandstone walls used lighter coloured stones for relief when forming borders for sections that were carved so realistically that the subject appeared natural.

Aerial view of Taj. On the opposite bank of the river are the ruins of an old foundation where Shah Jahan had intended to build a mausoleum for himself in black marble replicating Taj. But Aurangzeb, his parsimonious son, thwarted the plan.

Next page: Exquisite craftsmanship on marble at the Taj.

View of Taj Mahal from Khas Mahal in the Fort

Facing page: The Taj, as seen through the morning mist. 'The Taj is a poem. It is not only a pure architectural type, but also a creation which satisfies the imagination, because its characteristic is Beauty.'

Below: In the entire architectural scheme of the Taj, the actual tomb occupies a relatively small portion. The complex is in the form of a rectangle aligned north-south; in the centre is a square garden, leaving an oblong space at either end of the rectangle. In the south this is taken up by the gateway and the auxiliary buildings; in the north, along the silent river front, by the tomb itself.

Like most Moghul mausoleums, the Taj Mahal is a garden tomb. The site selected for the mausoleum was the garden of Raja Jai Singh of Jaipur. The spacious garden is laid out in the charbagh style (rectangle divided into four equal parts), with a spacious marble platform at the centre. A row of fountains placed some feet from each other is carried from end to end with a beautiful walkway on both sides. The Taj is situated at the end of the spacious charbagh.

The 24 carved marble fountains in the water-course stand silent as the Taj shimmers in the still sheet of water.

Below: Full view of the Taj.

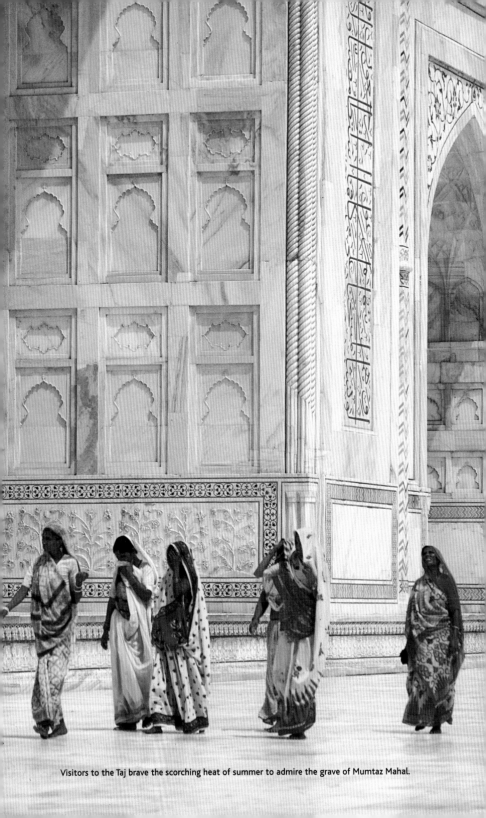

Visitors to the Taj brave the scorching heat of summer to admire the grave of Mumtaz Mahal.

The silhouette acquires a soft ephemeral glimmer with the approach of dusk.

may look for the relief on one of the riverside panels below the terrace.

The garden setting of a *rauza* is symbolic of the Bagh-i-Adan (Garden of Eden) of the Islamic paradise. A Hauz-i-Kausar and Tasneem expressed in the form of a central tank and channels of crystal clear running water, are essential features. The present lawns and gardens, though beautiful in themselves, were designed towards the end of the nineteenth century. In the Taj Museum, the visitor may see a wall-sized plan of the garden, consisting of plots of different kinds of fruits laid within the conventional *charbagh*. The emperor set apart the revenue of thirty villages for maintenance of the Taj and the charities he had ordained. This was supplemented by the income from the shops and stalls in the Jilau Khana, and the sale of fruit from the garden. Some of the income went towards the maintenance of the *khadims* (caretakers). Thus the Bagh-i-Adan had a practical purpose as well.

Proceeding along the axial water channel in the direction of the tomb, the visitor arrives at the elevated Hauz-i-Kausar (pool) in the centre of the garden. Four broad water channels, with fountains and double causeways on either side, radiate from the pool and divide the *charbagh* into four large quarters. Each of these is in turn exactly quartered, into sixteen parterres in all. Another innovation will be noticed from this central point. The east-west axial water channels end in Naubat Khanas (music houses) instead of the false gateways of the conventional *charbagh* plan. Musicians played their instruments in these pavilions when there was an *urs* and on Thursdays, to greet the arrival of the emperor on his weekly visits to the tomb. The Naubat Khanas are in red sandstone, designed and decorated with elegant simplicity, and crowned by marble domes. Beautiful views of the tomb and gardens can be had from the pavilions in the second storey.

Although the experience of the Taj is essentially aesthetic, the dimensions speak for themselves. Comparisons have been made with the plinth heights of other Mughal monuments. The Taj at 5.486 metres is thought to be an improvement on Humayun's tomb (6.71 metres) and Akbar's monument in Sikandra (9.14 metres). The latter, it must be remembered, stands directly on a large platform, and 9.14 metres represents the height of the first storey of the ascending pyramid. There is a truer parallel with Humayun's tomb. When viewed from the south the Taj could have done with a slightly higher terrace. The determining factor was probably the river view. Besides adding unconscionably to the weight, on foundations vulnerable to river action, a higher elevation would have created difficulties of perspective from the river, particularly in winter, when it is low. River conditions must also have been very carefully studied. As experience of the floods of 1924 and 1978 conclusively proved, the terrace always remains above high flood level. Aesthetic considerations were therefore based on sound engineering.

Externally, the mausoleum is a square, 56.9 metres each way. The corners are chamfered, and the cenotaph chamber rises in this form to a height of 32.92 metres along the top of the parapet over the entrance archway. The dome, resting on its drum, takes the mausoleum to a height of 74.22 metres at the crescent tip of its finial. Base to tip, the finial is 9.30 metres in height. The terrace on which the mausoleum stands is a square of 95.40 metres resting on a platform extending through the full breadth of the rectangle between the side walls. Slender and tapering minarets rise through the four corners of the terrace to a height of 41.76 metres, nearly reaching, though not exceeding, the widest horizontal section of the dome. The platform terminates in a mosque on the western side and its counterpart, the Mihman Khana, at the eastern end.

As the tomb is approached, the perception of its dimensions melts away in deepening awareness of the perfection of its proportions. Each element completely harmonises with the total composition. The minarets, for example, are detached from the funerary chamber and yet are integrally related to it. They are the *corps de ballet*, tenderly escorting the swan queen in their midst. Their refinement of line is no less elegant when seen by themselves. The three storeys are marked at each stage by discreet balconies, supported on Hindu brackets, and topped by dripstoned cupolas held aloft by eight finely proportioned columns. In contrast to rest of the mausoleum, the face joints of the finely cut marble blocks are countersunk and lined with black slate. Their simplicity enhances the beauty of the centrepiece of the whole arrangement, the tomb itself.

The highly successful mingling of Persian and indigenous features in the minarets is triumphantly demonstrated in the dome and its four attendant octagonal *chhattris*. These stand gracefully apart from the dome; there is no suggestion of congestion, as in Sher Shah's tomb in Sassaram. A single *chhattri* is placed over each chamfered corner, so that two

153

chhattris, aligned with the corresponding minarets, transect the other diagonal through the centre of the drum supporting the dome. And it is the onion dome which is the monument's crowning achievement. Percy Brown has drawn attention to an important aspect of which the visitor will soon become aware. From whichever angle the dome may be viewed, it is the central segment of a perfect globe. The lower part rests on the drum and the corresponding section above extends tangentially to the foliated base of a striking finial, reproduced in coloured slate embedded in the terrace to the east of the tomb. The inverted lotus and tapering *kalasa* (water pot), both indigenous symbols, harmonise perfectly with the crescent at the tip. Originally, the finial was sheathed in 44,000 tolas of pure gold. It was deprived of this beautiful covering by British troops, after they captured Agra from the Marathas in 1803.

The conception of the dome as a perfect sphere was apparently in the mind of Jahangir's architect, who had earlier designed the gemlike Moti Masjid in Lahore fort. It is in the Taj, however, that the idea is realised with brilliant success. Inside, the soffits soar to a height of 24.38 metres, thus leaving an immense hollow of about 36.58 metres between the two shells of the double dome, depending on their thickness. Although double domes had been used in churches and mosques in West Asia for several centuries, they were first tried in Hindustan by the Lodis early in the sixteenth century, notably in the tomb of Sikandar Lodi, who died in 1518.

The Taj dome is unquestionably the ultimate achievement in a development that started when the dome was first brought to Hindustan by the earliest Turkish rulers in the twelfth century. A double dome is essentially an architectural device to create the right proportions externally as well as in the interior. Mughal architects first experimented with it in Humayun's tomb. There is little doubt that in the 150 years which had passed since its introduction in Hindustan, the art had been mastered by Indian builders. Fatehpur furnishes clear evidence, though on a much smaller scale. Ismail Khan, the Turkish builder of the Taj dome, must have been assisted by a team of skilled Indian dome makers.

As the tomb is approached, the purpose of chamfering the corners will become evident: it is to relieve corner angularity and relate the minarets to the whole ensemble in a way that would not have been quite as happy had the structure remained a perfect square. But the architect also planned for sides in single planes to accommodate the conventional *aiwan*, flanked by pairs of recesses on either side, one above the other. In Humayun's tomb, the *aiwan* itself is recessed, while the chamfered features become full-fledged octagons that stand out beyond the facades on each side. The linear design of the Taj, cut away at the corners, makes for far greater simplicity. It also provides four planes that serve as frames for an unrivalled display of marble reliefs and pietra dura inlay.

The urge to decorate, however, does not overpower the designers, as it does in Chini ka rauza, across the river, and in Wazir Khan's mosque in Lahore. Both were constructed in roughly the same period. In these monuments, and a whole array of contemporary buildings, such as Chauburji in Lahore, tiled decoration took over to such an extent that the builders were committed to providing as much lain surface as possible. Mouldings and courses were often dispensed with altogether. The emphasis in the Taj is on unity of form. The pietra dura inlay, which here attains the supreme heights of fine art, lends itself to the poetry of form with far greater felicity than tiled decoration. Pietra dura causes less disturbance to surface planes and is also much stronger. It becomes an integral part of the marble veneer, while tiles are comparatively fragile pieces superimposed on the masonry base. Yet it is only when the visitor mounts the terrace that the decorations, which cover the whole surface up to the parapet, begin to suggest their presence. The impression of richness tempered by restraint is confirmed by the interior decorations as well.

A narrow stairway brings the visitor face to face with the supremely beautiful entrance to the tomb. Stalactites carry the soffit to the point of the arch, the whole formed in marble bands inscribed in black slate with Quranic texts by that unique master, Amanat Khan Shirazi. Evidence has been found that he was also the designer of the inscriptions in Akbar's tomb at Sikandra. Pietra dura inlay adorns the spandrels in flowing designs. Slender pilasters, with black and yellow chevron tessellations, spring upwards along the quoins beyond the parapet to end in open lotuses, each crowned with a tiny dome and finial. The recesses on either side are treated likewise, but these end in lower parapets, permitting views of the corner *chhattris,* which are only gradually covered as the tomb is approached.

The care with which the *mimar-i-kul* thought out this seemingly minor point is illustrated once again in the design of

the vertically paired recesses on either side of the *aiwan*. These
are rectangular, while those in the chamfered ends are semi-
octagons. Not only does this create variety and charm, but also
a wide angle to view the feature as one moves around the
corners. It is this attention to small detail which places the Taj
in a class of itself. The *mimar-i-kul* used subsidiary features,
such as *chhattris*, pilasters and decoration, only to the extent
that these served his compelling purpose of creating supreme
harmony of form.

The southern facade is repeated on the other three sides
without entrance doorways. While circling the monument, one
cannot fail to perceive the intimacy of its relationship with the
river. Unhappily, the river has been drained of much of its
flow, to feed the canals India needs just as much as splendid
monuments. It is nothing like as noble a stream as it was in
Shah Jahan's days, or even when Hodges and the Daniells
painted the scene from the opposite bank.

* * *

The tomb's internal arrangement accords with the traditional
Persian plan. The mortuary chamber is at ground level,
approached by a sloping ramp near the main entrance. The
cenotaphs have been placed in identical positions directly
above, Mumtaz Mahal's in the centre and Shah Jahan's to the
side, much more imposing in size, as befits his imperial station.
The vault 24.38 metres above, is drawn together in stalactite
soffits, scarcely visible in the dim light. There are rectangular
rooms on all four sides with domical chambers in the
chamfered corners. All these rooms are interconnected and

passages radiate from the centre to the corners. Selections from the Quran are intoned in these chambers by *huffaz* appointed for the purpose. Thus they are not a mere ambulatory, but serve an important devotional purpose. Enclosed within them, the cenotaph chamber becomes an octagon. Light reflected from the dazzling marble filters into the interior through double screens of marble on the inner and outer faces of the walls. The spaces are filled with slightly milky glass, the whole interior thus being known as Aina Mahal (Glass Palace).

The light in Aina Mahal creates effects in the decorated marble interior as magical as they are. Fretted screens, exquisitely carved out of complete blocks of white marble and set in frames of pietra dura inlay, form an octagon around the cenotaphs. This masterpiece alone took ten years to be made. The air of hushed solemnity inside the screens, embalmed in the lalique light of Aina Mahal, is better experienced than described.

Originally, the cenotaphs were enclosed by a gem-encrusted rail of solid gold. Abdul Hamid Lahori tells us that 40,000 *tolas* (466.550 kgs) of the metal were given for fabrication to Bebadal Khan, superintendent of the goldsmith's department. Bebadal Khan, it will be recalled, had also been entrusted with the fabrication of the celebrated Peacock Throne. In 1642, this extravagantly showy feature was replaced by the exquisite marble screen seen there today. Though the reason given is that the dazzling golden rail, decorated by priceless gems, would not have been proof against the cupidity of visitors, it can hardly be doubted that Shah Jahan's impeccable taste prevailed.

There are few sights in the Taj to rival the approach to the cenotaphs through the open archway of the fretted marble screen. Shah Jahan's cenotaph bears the stamp of the austere reigning emperor, Aurangzeb. He allowed his father a more imposing memorial than the empress', but Quranic texts are conspicuously absent. It is engraved in Nastaliq script with the date of his death, and all his resounding titles. The gravestone below is substantially similar.

Mumtaz Mahal's cenotaph has a descriptive line in Nastaliq and Quranic verses in Naskh. Down below, her gravestone is inscribed with the ninety-nine names of God in highly stylised Naskh characters. In the subdued light of the mortuary chamber, a torch may have to be flashed, though an oil lantern held aloft creates a far finer effect. All the artistry and skill of the designers and mosaic workers is lavished on the beautifully proportioned marble graves. Agate, bloodstone, lapis lazuli, carnelian and other stones are cut and laid in floral arabesques and carpet designs with such precision that it is difficult to distinguish each piece with the naked eye. There are as many as thirty-one distinct pieces in the poppy and sixty-four in the large flower on the outer side of the arch in the screen above.

While in the cenotaph chamber, one of the *huffaz* reciting passages from the Quran in a corner of Aina Mahal may be persuaded to intone 'Allah-hu-Akbar' in a mellow voice as only they know how. The sound resonates through the passages and the high domed vault, echoing back, if well performed, for as long as thirteen seconds. To hear it is itself a spiritual experience. Can it be that the divine chant was somehow embalmed forever in the vault above and that its chords are touched only by the invocation from below? In the beginning was the Word! The Taj unfolds its rarest experience for all who but hear the sound.

After such a sublime experience, anti-climax may be expected, but the marble reliefs and pietra dura inlays in the walls from the dados upwards, are decorated like so many miniature paintings. These arts had already been practised with consummate skill in the tomb of Itimad-ud-Daula. In the Taj they attain a perfection never rivalled, before or since. The relief of *guldastas* (vases), of flowers and foliage, framed in flowing designs executed in pietra dura, are the equivalent in marble and gems of Mughal miniatures of the post-Akbari school. The later work in Delhi fort lacks the same measure of refinement. In the Taj, Shah Jahan's sole commitment was to beauty; in Delhi the obsession was grand display. There is a distinct decline in discrimination and good taste.

The interior of the tomb was laid with sumptuous carpets, and decorated, as Tavernier says, with 'chandeliers and other ornaments of the kind, and there are always some *mullahs* there to pray.' He was evidently reporting only what he had heard, because he could not have been any luckier than Bernier, who frankly admitted he had never been allowed inside. Bernier adds: 'But I understand that nothing can be conceived more rich and magnificent.'

The Taj is distinguished by the provision of a mosque as a part of the *rauza*. An identical structure has been provided at the eastern end of the platform to balance the mosque, but lacking the special features of a mosque such as *mihrab* and *qibla.* This is sometimes called Jawab (answer), or Jamaat Khana (place of assembly) or Mihman Khana (guest house). The British chose to use it as an occasional residence and made some modifications inside. Though the mosque and Mihman Khana have distinct purposes, there is also excellent architectural justification for placing them where they are. Built predominantly of red sandstone, they are much smaller in scale than the Taj and nowhere near its equal in beauty. Thus, their artistic purpose is to set off the Taj and highlight its excellence.

The Taj, it must be remembered, is an *urs*, a place of pilgrimage and religious observances, but it is also a festal hall. What is meet may be done, though profane enjoyment would be utterly out of place. A hundred years ago, boys from the city laid bets on whose orange would stay up longest in the jets of water spouting from the fountains. The guardians of the souls in paradise must view restrained pleasures in the grounds of the eternal festal hall with benevolent tolerance.

* * *

Before they see an acknowledged wonder of the world, most people are psychologically, apt to prepare themselves for disappointment. Every visit to the Taj Mahal, however, is a new and deeper experience. As one passes through the domed hall of the portal, the Taj itself bursts into view. Appreciation is necessarily personal, but the dominant impression almost invariably is of the monument's matchless beauty and unrivalled harmony of proportion.

Seen as a whole, the Taj Mahal appears as an orchestration of three integrally related elements — the environment, in which the river and sky are the main components, the *charbagh* and the tomb itself, floating ethereally between and reflecting the ever-changing moods and colours of the sky. This grand conception could not have been anyone but Shah Jahan's. No *mimar-i-kul*, much less a visiting architect from Venice, Turkey or France, could have imposed this vision on the Grand Mughal planning a matchless festal chamber and last resting place for his devoted wife and himself. From childhood to his years as an aspiring heir, Shah Jahan must have looked out countless times from the palaces in the fort towards the gardens along the river. Is it too fanciful to suppose that he had pictured a festal hall of surpassing beauty on the river bank? When tragedy unexpectedly struck, the distant vision became an immediate need.

In a once-in-a–lifetime visit, it may be difficult to visualise the eternal communion of the Taj with its environment. The transient mood of the sky, the play of light and shade from passing clouds, morning, the fast changing colours of sunset, all subtly flow over the mouldings and soft contours. Though it may draw a heavy curtain across the sky, even torrential rain cannot conceal its beauty, while lightning creates flashing intensities in the marble forms, which are magical in their effect. On a full moon night, particularly the pearly blue of *sharad poornima* (usually the end of October), the semi-precious stones glow like myriads of fireflies. Unquestionably, the harmonies of form and environment, pulsating inseparably together, are the supreme achievement of the Taj.

From the southern gateway, the Taj Mahal appears as a

total composition, that for sheer harmony has few equals anywhere in the world. The monument, with its flanking mosque and Mihman Khana, were intended to be seen floating above the flowers, and fruit trees in the rainbow spray of the fountains playing between. As it is approached, the monument grows in size without the perfection of its proportions in any way being diminished. Indeed, wonder deepens, for the Taj passes the test of closer scrutiny from whichever angle it may be viewed.

The symmetry with which the masses — the funerary chamber, the dome, *chhattris*, finials and minarets — have been arranged, could have proved tiresome. It has been suggested, for instance, that the top line of the parapet above the apsed entrance to the tomb is the middle point in the whole elevation.[2] However, it is not a 1:1 relationship. The calculus is different. The *mimar-i-kul* apparently took account of the tapering effect of the onion dome as it reaches towards the finial. In allowing for this optical effect, the upper half seems taller than it actually is. The aim is always compositional harmony rather than the perfection of geometry as an end in itself; and nowhere have the rhythms of proportion been exemplified with such chaste distinction as in the disposition of the minarets.

Another, and no less important purpose of the arrangement of masses is to disperse the blinding dazzle of sunlight from pure white marble. The soft mouldings of the rounded dome and the contours of other features atop the funerary chamber effectively serve this purpose. A different treatment was necessary on plain surfaces. Here dazzle has been softened by skilful use of inlaid decoration. Shah Jahan could easily have succumbed to the temptation of display for its own sake, but the accusation of excess cannot conceivably be levelled at the decoration of his *chef d'oeuvre*; it never obtrudes. As the visitor approaches, he is hardly conscious of the wealth of the semi-precious stones inlaid in the marble and the artistry of design. To be sure, restraint in decoration is dictated by Islamic ideals.

Reactions to the Taj range from Aldous Huxley's intellectual disapproval in *Jesting Pilate* to Philip Wylie's tears, as he collapsed on the steps of the portal when the full view of the monument broke on him through the domed hall. Kruschev's dry comment that the Taj was a creation of slave labour, was an ideologically conditioned reflex based on misconceptions about the social and economic conditions of the times; it was not an appreciation of the monument itself. Each one to himself.

Much nearer the bone is V.S. Naipaul's visceral aversion: 'In India these endless mosques and rhetorical mausolea, these great palaces speak only of a personal plunder and a country with an infinite capacity for being plundered ... In India it (the Taj) is a building wastefully without a function, it is only a despot's monument to a woman, not of India, who bore a child every year for fifteen years.[3] A mosque is place of prayer, of dedication and self-purification of the *jamaat* (congregation). If Naipaul had tried to understand the experience of Islam, he might not have found 'these endless mosques' so irrelevant. By offering *nazrana* of jewels and precious stones, the princes and nobles became in some sense participants in the Taj as a symbol of the grandeur of the empire. It was in such phrases of stone and ornament that 'sun kings' expressed, what we have come to regard as the vanity of power. Nor can it be believed that the architects, designers, calligraphists, stone-workers, jewellers and builders did not experience the sheer joy of creation. Their work is too perfect to be no more than the mechanical product of 'personal plunder.' It is surely a profound misunderstanding to suppose that twenty-two years' labour by twenty thousand workers amounted to no more than a woman's gravestone. The woman, incidentally, was a third generation Persian Indian, and fairly typical of the evolving ruling class three and a half centuries ago.

When Lord Lake occupied Agra in 1803, his dragoons stripped the Taj's finial of its gleaming gold coating. These high-spirited fellows rounded off the day by digging out the best stones they could find in the pietra dura inlay. According to the book by JTN published in Lahore in 1862, the *khadims* insisted on telling visitors to the Taj that the stones had been stolen by Firangis. Their bitterness is understandable. These diversions were still in fashion at the end of the century when Lord Curzon wrote with acid sarcasm: 'It was not an uncommon thing for the revellers to arm themselves with hammer and chisel, with which they whiled away the afternoon by chipping out fragments of agate and carnelian from the cenotaphs of the Emperor and his lamented Queen.' The Jami Masjid, perhaps not an outstanding specimen of architecture, was adorned by a fine gateway, which was pulled down by the British along with the enclosed market with three gates called Tripolia. Only the name of the market has been preserved.

Today, the Taj itself is threatened by an invisible danger — the acrid vapours of industry. But it is immune from the criticism of social historians and peevish fault-finders. It belongs to an age of grandeur that is past, but it belongs also to the present — to the thousands of visitors from every corner of the world, frenetically clicking cameras, and the streams of Indians for whom a visit to this diadem of their own past has become a vivid experience of national unity. There is for all, yet the Taj is incomplete without the dazzling *lehngas* of Rajasthan, the brilliant *safas* of Punjabi Sikhs, the chequered *lungis* from the south, and the surging mass of people from all over the country, enlivening the forecourt, the radiating causeways, the rim of the lotus pool and the terrace of the tomb itself. This is the reenactment of the festal hall. Today, the *baradari* is not for the privileged enjoyment of vanished kings and emperors, but a moment of joy for the people of India and the world.

---

1   Dr G.A. Qamar's unpublished papers.

2   Percy Brown in *Indian Architecture* (The Islamic Period).

3   V.S. Naipaul in *An Area of Darkness.*

GROUND PLAN AND SECTION VIEW OF TAJ MAHAL

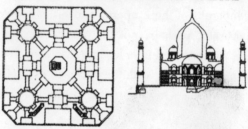